The Handgun of the Holy Ghost, Understanding the Spirit of God

❧

By Dr. James C. Warner

Xulon PRESS

The Handgun of the Holy Ghost
Understanding the Spirit of God
by Dr. James C. Warner

Printed in the United States of America

ISBN-13: 978-1-60034-841-9
ISBN-10: 1-60034-841-6

www.xulonpress.com

ACKNOWLEDGEMENTS

I would like to acknowledge the assistance of several people in helping me write this, my first, book. Thanks first to my wife Janet who encouraged me to continue in the writing and also helped me by engaging me with good conversation and questioning the different subjects.

Thanks to Rev. Tony Dan Helka for his helpful criticisms in making the book more "readable" and more acceptable to all readers. Thanks to Rev. David Osborn for his comments and direction in publishing. I want to thank Rev. Donald Lyon for keeping me theologically sound. And in addition, I thank Mr. Ivan Dremann for correcting several grammatical errors in my manuscript. Any errors still found are more than likely due to my missing his corrections.

King Solomon said that there was nothing new under the sun. The teachings in this book are not original. I acknowledge the teachings of many pastors and Bible teachers in forming my Biblical views. Special acknowledgement goes to the Teacher of the Church: the Holy Spirit of God.

Sincerely,

James C. Warner D.C.
September 26, 2006

Purpose

~≋~

Dear Reader.

I have a twofold purpose in writing this book on the Holy
Spirit.

1. To give honor to the Holy Spirit of God.
2. To teach accurately the Holy Spirit's relationship to
    the believer in Jesus Christ.

There are multitudes of books on the Holy Spirit. Many
are excellent and have enlightened me to the work of the
Holy Spirit and have given me the basis to write this book.
I claim no superiority over any other Spirit-led authors. I
humbly submit this study to you for your instruction, edifica-
tion, and success in ministry.

So why another book on the Holy Spirit? The reason is
that it has taken years of study and seeking for me to get
the answers contained herein. I have visited untold scores of
churches of various denominations, spoken with hundreds
of pastors, read volumes on the topic, and graduated from
seminary without benefit of this volume. I've had questions!
I still do!

Many Christian churches/denominations may have differences of opinion as to the Holy Spirit. Regardless of your church affiliation, this book will help you understand the Holy Spirit. You probably have not been taught these things in church. I ask you to be like the Bereans: that you receive the Word with readiness of mind, search the Scriptures daily, and find out if whether these things are true (Acts 17:11).

To write about the Holy Spirit (or Ghost if you prefer) is not taken lightly. I bow daily to the Spirit of God. I meet Him regularly in the Secret Place-my prayer closet if you will. I want only to honor my God and share some things He has taught me with others, that they might experience what I have. I have no axe to grind with anyone.

My intent is to base this volume only on the Bible-the Word of God. The various Scriptures may be highlighted and expounded with the comments and writings of people, along with my observations. Is this book without error? When you find a Bible reference-that verse is without error.

All scripture is given by inspiration of God, and is profitable for doctrine, for reproof, for correction, for instruction in righteousness: that the man of God may be perfect, thoroughly furnished unto all good works.

II Timothy 3:16

Dr. James C. Warner
jwarner@warnerchiro.com

TABLE OF CONTENTS

❦

Chapter 1.

DO YOU HAVE THE HOLY GHOST?

"Do you have the Holy Ghost?" was the question I was asked. This Pentecostal preacher knew his topic and I was nervous! Every week it was our practice to say the Apostles' Creed in my denominational church. I regularly proclaimed that Jesus "was conceived by the Holy Ghost" and that "I believe in the Holy Ghost." But to recite the Apostles' Creed was not what he was asking.

"What do you mean? I'm a Christian. We all have the Holy Ghost, don't we?" was my reply.

"Have you been baptized in the Name of Jesus and come out of the water speaking in tongues?" was the next question I was up against. This started me on the journey that led to this book. Maybe you have had similar exchanges with believers of various persuasions. How did you answer? Did you feel comfortable?

Do you have the Holy Ghost? That should not be a difficult question. Someone should be able to quickly say "yes" or "no." Why is it hard to answer and why is it so divisive a question?

Dear reader, if you are not a Christian the answer is a definite "no." The Bible clearly states, *"Now, if any man have not the Spirit of Christ, he is none of his."(Romans 8:9b)* If you don't have the Holy Spirit, you are not a child of God. You might say, but aren't we all children of God? Not according to the God of the Bible. St. John says it well, *"But as many as received him (the Spirit of Christ-author added) to them gave he power to become the sons of God..."* We are all created by God in His image, but we are not all sons. First we must receive Him!

Let's look at what Jesus said about this in John, chapter 3:

There was a man of the Pharisees, named Nicodemus, a ruler of the Jews:

The same came to Jesus by night, and said unto him, Rabbi, we know that thou art a teacher come from God: for no man can do these miracles that thou doest, except God be with him.

Jesus answered and said unto him, Verily, verily, I say unto thee, Except a man be born again, he cannot see the kingdom of God.

Nicodemus saith unto him, How can a man be born when he is old? Can he enter the second time into his mother's womb, and be born?

Jesus answered, Verily, verily, I say unto thee, Except a man be born of water and of the Spirit, he cannot enter into the kingdom of God.

That which is born of the flesh is flesh; and that which is born of the Spirit is spirit.

Marvel not that I said unto thee, Ye must be born again.

Dear reader, Jesus said you must be born again or you wouldn't even be able to "see" the kingdom of God. You wouldn't be able to understand or comprehend the things of God. That is why some things you just don't "get." Life is confusing when we don't understand what is going on.

Millions of people go to church and aren't born again. Church is boring for them. Reading the Bible can be difficult for you.

I have heard priests and pastors say, "We don't go along with that 'born again' stuff." If you have been told that, the person who told you was one of those who doesn't "get" it. I don't care how many theological degrees they have. Nicodemus was a Pharisee, a ruler of the Jews. He had all the degrees and labels. But Jesus told him, "You must be born again." It is a message that Jesus tells every rabbi, priest, and pastor today. Everybody must be born again.

Nicodemus didn't get it. He asked, *"How can a man be born when he is old?"* Notice he didn't argue with Jesus. He honestly asked because he didn't know. When we come to Jesus with an honest question, he will always come to the aid of our ignorance and teach what we need to know. Jesus isn't trying to keep anyone out of His Kingdom, whether that person is a Jew or Gentile. To the contrary, He went to the cross so that "anyone" could enter His Kingdom.

Jesus next says that a person must be born of water and of the Spirit, or that person cannot *enter* into the Kingdom of God. The entrance into the Kingdom of God is through the second birth, which is of the Spirit. The first birth is when we are born physically, or of the flesh (verse 6). This is a water birth as anyone who has had a child can tell! When that bag of water bursts the long awaited child is about to enter this world. To be born again is the Spiritual birth. *"That which is born of the Spirit is spirit,"* said Jesus (verse 6). When that person is born spiritually the long awaited person becomes a child of God and enters the Kingdom of God. You cannot just be born once and see or enter the Kingdom of God; you MUST be born *again*. There is no other way.

I suppose the next question one may ask is what does it mean to be born of the Spirit. Being born of the Spirit means

13

to have the Holy Ghost (or Spirit of Christ) come inside you. This is called the New Birth, or born again. Obviously, if the Holy Spirit was inside of you, you would have the Holy Ghost. If He was not inside you, you wouldn't have the Holy Ghost. Simple, isn't it?

The Bible has other words to describe the experience: words like salvation, being saved, and others. If you have salvation, you have entered into the Kingdom. If you are saved (which is from sin, hell, and the devil), you are born of the Spirit. This occurs when someone repents, confesses his or her sins, and asks Jesus to come into them. Obviously, Jesus doesn't BODILY enter into someone, so His Spirit comes into his or her body. That person should then follow in baptism. Baptism (which will be dealt with in later chapters) is a picture of the death, burial, and resurrection of Jesus Christ. This entire process is the work of the Holy Spirit. It is the Spirit of the Father that *draws* the unbeliever to salvation (John 6:44).

Romans 6:4 says, *"Therefore we are buried with him by baptism into death; that like as Christ was raised up from the dead by the glory of the Father, even so we also should walk in newness of life."* Baptism is a physical acting out of our old, sinful self dying, being buried (placed under water) and raising (coming up from the water) from the dead. It was the Holy Spirit who raised Jesus from the dead and it is the Holy Spirit that raises us from the dead!

Romans 8:11, *"But if the Spirit of him that raised up Jesus from the dead dwell in you, he that raised up Christ from the dead shall also quicken your mortal bodies by his Spirit that dwelleth in you."* You were dead-now you are alive! Sin brings death, but the Spirit brings life. You now have eternal life because the eternal One lives in you. You are born again, in the Kingdom of God, saved, the Spirit of God living in you! You are not the same. You are a new creation:

"Therefore, if any man be in Christ, he is a new creature: old things are passed away; behold, all things are become new." (II Corinthians 5:17).

That is why Peter boldly proclaimed on the day of Pentecost to thousands, *"Repent, and be baptized every one of you in the name of Jesus Christ for the remission of sins, and ye shall receive the gift of the Holy Ghost." (Acts 2:38).* Please notice repentance always comes before baptism in the Bible. One repents to become a Christian. It is part of the belief process. Christians are baptized. One does not become a Christian by baptism. In every instance in the Bible, repentance/belief always came first. Jesus said to believe and be baptized and you will be saved, belief coming first (Mark 16:16). He also said to make disciples and then baptize them (Matthew 28:19). If you were taught that baptism came first, it was from a well-meaning person who had it backwards. Remember the Bereans, and search the Scriptures to see if that isn't so.

Berea was a city in Macedonia where Paul and Silas traveled. The Bible calls its inhabitants noble, *in that they received the word with all readiness of mind, and searched the scriptures daily, whether those things were so (Acts 17:11).* The believers in Berea made sure even Paul and Silas had the Gospel right! Become a modern-day Berean, and see if you are being taught the truth.

Dear friend, do you want to be born of the Spirit? Repeat after me:

Dear God, I know that I am a sinner. I have sinned against you and others in thought, word and deed. I am sorry. I do ask you for forgiveness, as I no longer want to sin against you and others. Come into my life, Spirit of Christ, and make me a new creature, and I will live to serve you.

Friend, if you meant the above prayer, you are now born of the Spirit and can answer "yes" to "Do you have the Holy Ghost?" Follow in baptism. Remember Peter's declaration, "Repent, and be baptized." You are now ready to "see" the Kingdom of God and understand what is to follow.

Note: For some people this is a difficult chapter. I know. My family tradition and church background had it backwards-maybe for hundreds of years! It was a major decision in my life to choose to place the Bible ahead of any tradition. It was a decision I have never regretted. In Mark 7:13, Jesus said that some of our traditions cancel or negate the Word of God. I do not want anything in my life to negate God's Word for me. Sometimes following Jesus can be difficult in and out of church! Dear reader, do you have the Holy Ghost?

Chapter 2

IS THE HOLY GHOST GOD, OR THE POWER OF GOD?

⤎⤏

The person at my door was very persistent. He and the person with him were from a local "Kingdom Hall" and seemed to be speaking of a kingdom different from the one Jesus spoke of in John 3. They were well trained to follow a prepared script and I was busy doing something when the doorbell rang. They had the initial advantage.

"Good morning sir. Are you concerned about where the world is headed in these times?" was their initial question. They were ready for my yes or no answer. From this question the two went on to the next part of their outline and it looked like I was to be their next victim. I decided to throw them off with my Pentecostal friend's question, "Do you have the Holy Ghost?" One of the two immediately became quiet, letting me know that this one was the student, or learner, while the other was the "minister."

After their initial distress, I was told that the Holy Spirit was Jehovah's moving force. The Holy Spirit was a kind of power but definitely not Jehovah or God. After all, they said, the Holy Trinity was a pagan belief that they had rejected.

They even showed me that from one of their books that explained the Scriptures to them.

"Excuse me. Could I go get my Bible?" I went to get a Bible that did not come from any Watchtower publisher and I prayed that the Holy Spirit would take over this conversation. I returned with my Bible which had my notes written down about the Holy Spirit.

"Could we turn to Acts 5, verses 3 and 4?" I asked.

But Peter said, Ananias, why hath Satan filled thine heart to lie to the Holy Ghost.....thou hast not lied unto men, but unto God.

After reading it I said that the Bible teaches that to lie to the Holy Spirit is to lie to God. One can lie to only another being, not to a force or power. "Perhaps you need to re-evaluate what you have been taught. I have fifty other verses here I think we need to go over which talk about the Holy Spirit being a person and God (or Jehovah)." The student looked towards the "minister" with a look like, "What are we going to do now?" The "minister" could see this wasn't part of their prepared outline and they said good-bye. As they were leaving my property, I wished them well and said, "Remember, *there are three that bear record in heaven, the Father, the Word, and the Holy Ghost: and these three are one.* You can find this in 1 John 5:7." They didn't appreciate hearing about the Holy Spirit or the Holy Trinity. Their tradition made the Word of God of no effect (Matthew 15:6, Mark 7:13).

Let's talk about the Holy Spirit. From the previous chapter, we learned that if you are born again, you have the Holy Spirit living inside of you. If He is inside of you, you need to know and appreciate who that is in you!

The word "Holy" means to separate, or set apart by Biblical definition. Webster defines it for our purposes as belonging to or coming from God, consecrated, sacred, sinless, saintly, deserving deep respect: awe, adoration, and reverence.

The Word "Spirit" means breath or wind in the Hebrew and Greek languages. These are the languages in which the Bible was written. The word "Ghost" which is used interchangeably in the book means the same as Spirit. When the King James Version of the Bible was translated from Greek and Hebrew, the word Ghost was more commonly used than today. When the world thinks of a ghost, even now we can call it a spirit or something floating in the air. Since much of the time I will use the King James Version, the words "Holy Ghost" will mean the same as Holy Spirit, which is found also in the King James but always in newer translations.

The word spirit or ghost comes from the Greek word *pneuma*, from which we get the word pneumonia. We still use the old Biblical words "give up the ghost" for those who have breathed their last. It seems that with the final expiration the air leaves and it is rendered that the ghost/spirit left.

So we can confidently say that the Holy Spirit is the breath or wind that is sacred, sinless, belonging to and coming from God, and something to be held in awe and adoration. No wonder it is the Holy Spirit that gives life! No wonder it is the Holy Spirit with whom we are born again and given new life.

"For the law of the Spirit of life in Christ Jesus hath made me free from the law of sin and death."
Romans 8:2

I have heard and read that a major Christian denomination claims that the early church made up the concept of the Holy Spirit. According to this view, early Christians felt so bad about Jesus leaving them that they had to come up with a new doctrine to fill the gap! This is another example of tradition negating the Word of God. The Holy Spirit was first mentioned in the Bible at the very beginning: Genesis 1, verse 2.

And the earth was without form, and void; and darkness was upon the face of the deep. And the Spirit of God moved upon the face of the waters.

Dear reader, this was thousands of years before any denominational meeting came up with their brilliant beginning of the Holy Spirit.

If one doesn't believe in the Holy Spirit, he/she can't have the Holy Spirit. But the fact that some don't believe in the Holy Spirit does not mean there isn't one! I can jump off the bridge sincerely believing there is no such thing as gravity, but it doesn't change the fact of gravity. Some so-called Christian leaders have jumped off the bridge. They are the blind leading the blind. Jesus said:

"Let them alone. They are blind leaders of the blind. And if the blind leads the blind, both will fall into a ditch."

Matthew 15:14 NKJV

Let's get back to the original question, which was "Is the Holy Ghost God or the power of God?" The answer is "Yes." I would probably be correct in thinking that you felt you had to give an either/or answer. The Jehovah's Witnesses are correct when saying that the Holy Spirit is the power of God, but only half correct. And a half-truth is the same as a whole lie. If one doesn't believe in the Father, Son, and Holy Ghost as being the one true God, then the Holy Ghost will always mean something less than God, and therefore must be an attribute of God in their way of thinking. Let me illustrate it another way:

"For God so loved the world, that he gave his only begotten Son, that whosoever believeth in him shall not perish, but have everlasting life."

John 3:16

Here Jesus teaches that God loves the world, including the sinner. This shows a force or power (love) emanating from God toward something, like the object of His love or affection. To say that love is a power of God is correct, but not totally.

> *"He that loveth not knoweth not God; for God is love."*
>
> *I John 4:8*

God is love. That is what He is. Now God is more than love, but He is love. He is love, He has love, He gives love, and He loves! The fact that He is love and that He has love is just as true as the Holy Ghost being God and being the power of God. The power of love is the Holy Ghost too. The Father loves, the Son loves, and the Holy Spirit loves. I love because the Holy Spirit (love) is in me. Look up in Strong's or Young's Concordance the word love and see how often it is attributed to the Father, Son, and the Holy Ghost. All Three are Love and all Three love!

From the above Scripture, we can't know God if we don't love, because God is love. If God is love, when He comes into you in the form of the Holy Spirit, love is now inside you. Now you can know Him and love others including Him, as without Him you are not even able to love Him.

> *"We love him, because he first loved us."*
> *I John 4:19*

Isn't it great to love God and others, and know it is only because of Him? We had nothing to brag about! It's only because of Him. Before becoming a Christian, I used to have affection for others and for God, but not the Agape love of

God. Even the old affection or love I thought I had was only because He put that in me, even without actually abiding in me. Now He brought love into my heart that is so powerful, so that I can love Him and you with a never-ending love. Hallelujah! (Which means Praise the Lord!)

> *"God is spirit, and those who worship Him must worship in spirit and truth."*
>
> *John 4:24 NKJV*

The Holy Spirit is God. If you ever get a knock on the door by someone who doesn't think so, here are a few verses to help out.

Holy Spirit called God:	Acts 5:3,4, Romans 15:13, Hebrews 10:16, Ephesians 2:22
Called a Person:	John 16:7, Romans 8:11, I Peter 1:11
Called Lord	2 Corinthians 3:17,18
Called Comforter	John 14:16, 15:26, 16:7

His Attributes

Eternal	Hebrews 9:14
Omnipresent	Psalm 139:7
Omniscient:	1 Corinthians 2:10,11
All Powerful	Luke 1:35
Creator	Genesis 1
Gives Life	Romans 8:11, Genesis 2:7

His Actions

Speaks	Acts 1:16, 13:2, Hebrews 3:7, 10:15, Revelation 2:7, 22:17

Leads	Acts 8:29, Romans 8:14
Forbids	Acts 16:6,7
Reveals	1 Corinthians 2:9,10, 1 Peter 1:11
Intercedes	Romans 8:26
Testifies	John 15:26
Guides	John 16:13
Teaches	1 Corinthians 2:13
Carries	2 Peter 1:21
Gives Plans	1 Chronicles 28:12
Predicts	1 Peter 1:11
Gives Gifts	1 Corinthians 12:11
Searches	1 Corinthians 2:10
Convicts	John 16:8-11
Regenerates	John 3:5, Titus 3:5
Witnesses	Hebrews 10:15,16
Gives Opinions	Acts 15:28
Sends	Acts 10:19,20
Dwells	Romans 8:11
Baptizes	1 Corinthians 12:13

He Can Be

Lied to	Acts 5:3,4
Insulted	Hebrews 10:29
Grieved	Ephesians 4:30
Blasphemed	Matthew 12:31,32

Chapter 3

DRAWN BY THE
SPIRIT-MY TESTIMONY

I was raised in a family that believed there was a God. From my earliest recollections my mother prayed with me every night before bed. We prayed a common German prayer that kids say. I learned this in German not even knowing what I was saying. It was the first prayer I learned and I knew God knew what I was saying even if I didn't! From my earliest memories I always believed that there was a God and that He heard my prayer.

Ich bin klein,	I am small,
Mein Herz macht rein.	Make my heart clean.
Darf Niemand drin wohnen	Permit nothing to live inside
Als Jesus allein. Amen	But Jesus alone. Amen

As I grew older I continued saying my prayer regularly, but was not getting any benefit of church as my parents didn't attend. It wasn't until I was in first or second grade that a neighbor lady started taking me to church with her kids. I thank God for her, as without Mrs. Kilgore I would have had no church upbringing. As I grew older I was confirmed in this church after a year of regular classes on Saturdays. I continued attending the church till I was around 15 or so. Many ribbons and awards were given to me for good attendance. I know I went at least 1 year without missing a Sunday. I learned much about God and now said the Lord's Prayer daily, saying the German prayer less and less. I even considered the possibility of becoming a pastor when "grown up."

I give you this background to acknowledge that I had a religious background. I believed in the Virgin Birth. I believed that Jesus died for my sins. I had a conscience that alerted me when I did wrong. Other than humorous pranks that I did (and continue to do), most people would say I was a good example of an American Christian boy.

My teenage years were in the 1960's, a time of turbulence in our nation's history that has never been resolved to this day. My denomination became involved in what I considered the wrong side on some issues. I became upset and quit going to church. Besides, I was a teenager now and said, "You don't have to go to church to believe in God." How many times have you heard or said that line?

It was about this time that I was invited by a fellow student to a "revival" at his church. I attended with a couple of friends from my church and we were in for something we hadn't experienced before. Not only was sin preached against, but also pressure was put on us to "come forward" to be "saved." I wasn't sure I wanted to be "saved," but I sure didn't want to go to hell, which was the alternative. So I went forward scared and my knees "aknocking!" A counselor met me and took my friends and me to a separate room where it was explained what this was all about and prayers were said. This was totally new for my friends and me, and we were somewhat confused to say the least.

I felt God's presence during this service, but was mostly scared. I'm sure some seeds were definitely planted in me that night, but I still stayed away from church and eventually began to turn my back on God, still praying every night before bed. Soon I was out of high school, drinking and getting involved in situations I should have known better. I was now attending college and living a lifestyle I certainly wouldn't want my children to do. My grades were good, as I did very well in school. I was the self-sufficient, confident person who could handle any problem. I studied hard, worked hard, and played hard.

It was during my fourth year of college that I got engaged to a woman who had a child from a previous marriage. I thought I had found the right person for me. She had a similar background. We were engaged for eight months and the wedding date soon approached. Three days before the wedding we got in a big argument! I marched out of the house and later that night went to my bachelor's party. There was a lot of drinking, card playing, and cussing; but I was the only one not having any fun. I started having big doubts if I should get married. Turmoil was raising up within me. Should I or shouldn't I? All my friends were joking about me getting hitched, but I wasn't laughing. I stated that I had doubts, but was assured that this was normal. I was just a little nervous.

I left the party to spend the night with a friend, not wanting my fiancée to find me. I could not sleep at all that night and finally left his house at 3:00 or 4:00 in the morning. I drove to a large park and got out of my car and started walking around. Now was the time to get serious. I started talking to God about my life. "God, tell me what to do! Should I marry her or not? And what can we do about her quitting her job and the two of us renting an apartment 100 miles away?" In desperation, I got down on my knees next to a tree in Page Park, at 6:00 a.m. in the morning and cried out to God.

I confessed my sins to Him. I asked for forgiveness. I then said something to the Lord I never had before. I asked Jesus to come into me and make me a new person. I admitted that I had goofed up my life and that I wanted Him to take over. Whatever He told me to do, I would be willing to do. "Whatever you want me to do, marry her or not, I will do. Please make it plain, Lord." A strange feeling came over me. I got up on my feet and I was different. A load was lifted and I felt cleansed. I immediately had a different direction to go. I was now going to serve the Lord, no matter what. In my mind God had spoken and I was not to marry this woman. At that point there was a LOT of marriage plans that needed changing, and still a lot of tears. But I had a new life (years later we both married other people). Though this happened in 1974, my zeal for the Lord Jesus Christ has not diminished. God has blessed me way beyond my earlier imaginations. When I decided to follow His plan, I found my plans were insignificant. He had another woman in store for me, with 4 wonderful children that were soon added. Not only did I marry a Christian girl, but my children, parents, sister and her family have all received Christ as their personal savior. How did God do this?

By His Holy Spirit. Dear reader, I have given my testimony to show how the Holy Spirit of God brought me into the Kingdom. You should have a testimony also. If you have no testimony, maybe up to now you have fought the Holy Ghost just like I did.

For God so loved the world, that He gave His only Begotten Son, that whosoever believeth in Him should not perish, but have everlasting life.

John 3:16

God loves the world and everyone in the world, the lovely and the unlovely. God has an everlasting love that knows no bounds. He loves you and me to the point of sacrificing His only begotten (not made) Son. He sent Jesus to die for the sins you and I committed and still commit. Jesus got what we deserve and deserved. Dear reader, you and I were not so lily pure even at out best! Yet He loved us still. So Jesus shed His blood on the cross to pay for the sins we committed. His payment was in full. Nothing we could ever add to His sacrifice could pay for any sin. Anything we can try to add will only detract. The name of any person or the name of any religion cannot and will not ever save anybody:

> *Neither is there salvation in any other: for there is none other name under heaven given among men, whereby we must be saved.*
>
> *Acts 4:12*

We can only call upon the name of Jesus to save us.

> *For whosoever shall call upon the name of the Lord shall be saved.*
>
> *Romans 10:13*

While the Lord sent His Son to die for us, this act of love was for "whosoever," anyone who will. God is

> *…. longsuffering to us-ward, not willing that any should perish, but that all should come to repentance.*
>
> *II Peter 3:9*

It is God's desire that all people everywhere would repent and come to Him. He knows that nobody can on their own. That is where the Holy Spirit steps in. Since we cannot on our own merit claim any part in our salvation, the Holy Spirit takes it upon Himself to draw people to Him. Remember the scripture:

We love him, because he first loved us.

1 John 4:19

So how does the Holy Spirit draw people to Christ? He does it by a process called revelation. God reveals Himself to men and women, boys and girls by general revelation and specific revelation. General revelation is taught throughout the Bible. In Psalms the Bible states that "the heavens declare the glory of our God." The whole world shows that there was a divine Creator of the creation. Every country and every race of people have always acknowledged a supreme deity that ruled the affairs of men. This has gone on since the beginning of Man and has only had doubters in the last couple of centuries. Man has only recently gotten so smart that he doesn't want to say there is a God. The fact that people doubt God in their own minds does not mean God hasn't tried to show Himself to them.

Because that which may be known of God is manifest in them; for God hath shewed it unto them. For the invisible things of him from the creation of the world are clearly seen, being understood by the things that are made, even his eternal power and Godhead; so that they are without excuse.

Romans 1:19,20

There is no excuse for not knowing that there is a God! In my testimony I stated that I knew there was a God from my earliest memories. My parents taught me all I knew about God till I was able to learn more. God put me in an environment where I could respond to Him, one way or another. God was not trying to keep anything away from me. He showed me a large wonderful earth and said in effect, "This beautiful planet is to show you who I am. Enjoy it and come close to Me. I have so much for you." The wonders of nature

30

are a clear signature of God. All living on the face of the earth have experienced God's general revelation. God has revealed Himself in nature, physics, mathematics, science, and history: so to deny God is a form of disobedience to Him. That is why people who deny God are *"without excuse."*

The second method of revelation God uses is special revelation. The Bible and Jesus Himself are special revelation. Special revelation is when God does something over and above nature to show Himself to us. When Mrs. Kilgore took me to church, I heard words spoken in Sunday School and from the pulpit, which spoke of Jesus Christ, His death on the cross, and His resurrection. I was introduced to the Bible, the Word of God. When someone receives Special Revelation, it always leads to Jesus, the only name under heaven by which we must be saved. God revealed Himself to me when I went forward at the "revival." He was showing Himself to me, wanting me to accept Him totally. But I didn't respond as I should have and as He wanted. But God kept on trying! He didn't give up, even when I did! Faith was coming.

So then faith cometh by hearing, and hearing by the Word of God.

Romans 10:17

These words of faith were planted into me like seeds. Mark 4 talks about the sower planting seeds to get a harvest. Seeds being the Word of God, Mrs. Kilgore, my Sunday School teachers, pastors, etc. all planted and watered the seed in my life till the plant sprouted up. God used people to plant His Word into me. God took the initiative. I had certainly nothing to claim for my salvation coming to me.

31

For by grace are ye saved through faith; and that not of yourselves: it is the gift of God: not of works, lest any man should boast.

Ephesians 2:8,9

Grace is unmerited favor of God. It is a gift of God. General and Special Revelation is God's gift to us. God's revelation gives us the faith to receive His grace. His grace tells me that I am not guilty anymore for my sins. Jesus paid the penalty. But it is only available to those who receive it by faith. So in effect God gives us faith so that we can receive His grace. It's nothing we worked for and nothing we can brag about. His grace is for *whoever:* you and me.

Some would say His grace is irresistible, that when God calls people will always reply in the affirmative. If this were true, nobody would go to hell because Jesus died for the sins of the whole world. *God so loved the world that He gave His only begotten Son....* Remember the rich young ruler. Jesus said to give to the poor and follow Him. He offered the man His grace, but the man resisted and went away sad (Luke 18:18-23). The man felt he needed no repentance. In effect he was boasting that he had kept all the commandments. Can you imagine standing in front of Jesus, and saying, "I am a good person. I don't do anything wrong. I am as good as those church goers." And yet you and I have heard people say the same thing, with the same results as this young man. The Holy Spirit is trying to draw them but they resist Him. There can never be salvation till people stop resisting the Holy Spirit.

Sometimes the Holy Spirit calls and offers His grace but people want to receive it on their terms, not God's. John the Baptist was preaching in the wilderness saying:

Repent ye: for the kingdom of heaven is at hand...
Then went out to him Jerusalem, and all Judea, and
all the region round about Jordan, And were baptized

32

of him in Jordan, confessing their sins. But when he saw many of the Pharisees and Sadducces come to his baptism, he said unto them, O generation of vipers, who hath warned you to flee from the wrath to come? Bring forth therefore fruits meet for repentance:

Matthew 3:2-8

The Holy Spirit, through John, was calling people to repent and be baptized. Yet the religious leaders resisted the Spirit. They were good enough and didn't need to repent. "Just baptize me please." John sent them off till they were willing to accept what God wanted for them. The religious leaders came to John to show their religiosity, but not because the Spirit was drawing them. They may have felt a pull from God, but were too proud to confess their own sins. We could say they came to church for the wrong reasons and weren't about to change. Some Pharisees did eventually repent and come to God. Some came to Jesus and were converted. Nicodemus was one.

Jesus said, *"No man can come to me, except the Father which hath sent me draw him: and I will raise him up at the last day."*

John 6:44

Friend, you and I could never come to Jesus and His salvation unless the Father through His Spirit drew us. If we don't resist this drawing, then we are assured that Jesus Himself will raise you and I up at the last day. All we need do is just respond! Accept the free gift!

The wages of sin is death; but the gift of God is eternal life through Jesus Christ our Lord.

Romans 6:23

Sin will kill us but His free gift gives us eternal life. Jesus Himself promises to raise us up. Not only will we then live forever with Him, but our eternal life begins at the moment of our acceptance of the grace. I have eternal life now because the Eternal One lives inside me. When I die I just change geographical locations; but my spirit is alive, never more to die.

In my testimony I related how in my rebellious teenage years I ran from God. I didn't need Him and I didn't want to follow His rules. It bothered me when I did something against Him or others, but after much repetition one starts to harden. My rebellion took me to the point where I found myself incapable of fixing my situation. God did not want me to sin; however He allowed me to get myself in trouble. When I hit bottom He was there to offer me the free gift. It was almost like He said, "Have you had enough of your own ways? Why don't you quit arguing with me and do the right thing! My ways will only bring you life, yours will only lead to death." I received the free gift and became His child.

> But as many as received Him, to them gave He power to become the sons of God, even to them that believe on his Name.
>
> *John 1:12*

The Spirit drew me and now I am a child of the King. Dear reader, have you felt the drawing of the Holy Spirit and have you received the free gift of grace? If not, what are you waiting for? Repent and believe the Gospel!

Prayer: Dear God, thank-you for sending your Spirit to draw me to you. I confess my sins (name them to God), ask for forgiveness because of what Jesus did on the cross for me, and ask you Holy Spirit of God to dwell inside of me. Thank-you for coming in and granting me eternal life. In Jesus' Name, Amen.

Chapter 4

DOES WATER BAPTISM BRING ONE THE HOLY GHOST?

A fter experiencing the born-again event, God was moving mightily in my life. A hunger for the Bible, the Word of God, developed in me so that I read God's Word daily, a practice that has continued to this day. I also was impressed to return to church. Seeing I was back in college, I visited a church that was close to my school. The reason I went was because it was the closest to my apartment. I did not know what different denominations taught, or any of their specific doctrines.

I was soon going to weekly instruction classes and learning much about the Christian faith and church membership. The next to the last evening of classes the pastor wanted every student to be ready for the upcoming church service when the new members were inducted. It was at this time that the big question was asked of the prospective members.

"Were you baptized?" the pastor asked us.

"Yes, I believe I was," came my reply.

"You believe you were. You mean you don't know?" he asked.

"Well, my mother has always said I had been. But I don't remember, because I was only a baby."

"You need to find out for sure. You can't really be saved or join the church unless you have been baptized. You go to your mother and find out for sure. It can be a question of heaven or hell," he replied.

Now I was in a quandary. My eternal salvation was hanging on the line, and I had to trust my mother's word that I was baptized. In Germany, where I was born, the babies were often baptized in the hospital. You were baptized either Catholic or Protestant. My mother said I was baptized Protestant.

"Are you sure, Mom? I need to know for certain," I asked.

"Yes, I'm sure!" was her reply.

"Did you actually see the pastor do it?"

"Yes I did," she said.

"Well, do we have any proof? You know, a picture of it happening?"

"We don't have a picture. But I 'm sure we have a certificate packed away that proves it," she said.

To make a long story short, we could not find the certificate, but I went back to the pastor and assured him that my mother had me baptized. I became a member in good standing. But a little doubt was planted in my mind. Could it be that my eternal salvation was based upon my mother? My mother is a saint. She would never lie to me. But what if she was mistaken; or what if the pastor didn't say all the words correctly? Would God send me to hell for that? And should I go through life with this little speck of doubt hanging over me? Did something someone did to or for me decide if I were to go to heaven? And since I was only an infant, did I have no choice in the matter?

I was soon to learn that my church and denomination taught that baptism saves the person baptized, and that baptism was a "means of grace," a means that God used to impart saving grace into the baby. If an unbaptized baby was in the hospital near death, instructions are there so that anyone can baptize in an emergency to keep the child from hell. I accepted what was taught but began to question this doctrine. It sounded good, but certain Christians I met were talking about being born again and that didn't fit into my theology. I was reading the Bible regularly and various other Christian books and started to wonder what my church taught about that subject. Also, when did someone in my denomination receive the Holy Ghost? I thought that possibly the baby was saved when baptized and received the Holy Ghost when confirmed (Confirmed means to be confirmed into the faith.) I was soon to find out.

"Pastor, what is the church teaching on when someone receives the Holy Spirit? Is it at confirmation?" I asked.

"No; it's when the person (baby) is baptized. That is when the Holy Spirit enters the child and the child is then born again," he answered.

"You mean, the Holy Spirit comes in without the child's knowledge?" I asked.

"Yes, that is why there are parents and sponsors (godparents) who answer for the child and promise to raise the child in a Christian household. They enter into the baptismal covenant which the child confirms when older."

"Did it ever happen like that in the Bible?" I asked.

"Sure it did. It never says not to baptize babies. And Jesus said in Mark 10:14, *'Suffer the little children to come unto me, and forbid them not, for of such is the Kingdom of God.'* When we bring the babies to Him in baptism they are ushered into the Kingdom of God."

"I'm a little confused, pastor," I replied. "I know when I gave my life to Christ. It wasn't until 22 years after I was baptized."

"No," he said. "You received the Holy Spirit when a baby. That is when you were saved. You just realized it later on."

"You mean I was saved all along and never knew it?"

"Yes, God's saving grace and faith were imparted by baptism."

"Well, what about Hitler, Mussolini, and Stalin? They were all baptized as babies. Did they all have the Holy Spirit living in them? Were they saved? Did they go to heaven?" I inquired.

"I don't know," he countered. "They may have at some point refused the grace given to them at baptism. Martin Luther said to remember your baptism daily. They obviously didn't."

I again accepted my pastor's explanation, but decided to study up on the matter. My study eventually led to the concordance to see every passage of scripture that dealt with baptism. I asked myself if any passage on baptism I saw ever pertained to children or unbelievers. Surely the Bible would settle this for me! After all, my pastor knew the Bible a lot better than I did. And also, wasn't God's saving grace available to all? Couldn't I have had His grace all along and didn't know it, since it came when I was newly born? You know God is amazing and can do all things. Maybe He gave me His Spirit and I shouldn't question it. Was I being ungrateful, or un-Christian to wonder?

Dear reader, again be a Berean, and search the scriptures to find out if these things are true.

Chapter 5

BRING THE CHILDREN TO JESUS

❦

One of the most common passages when baptizing babies in my church was taken from the three synoptic Gospels (Matthew 19:14, Mark 10:14, and Luke 18:16). Jesus said,

> *"Suffer (permit) the little children to come unto me, and forbid them not: for of such is the Kingdom of God."*

This was often part of the liturgy said during the actual service. It sounded like Jesus wanted the children baptized. I went along with the liturgy, never questioning the church, pastor, or the scripture quoted. The problem is that in NONE of the three passages did the word baptize even exist. When studying Holy Scripture one is admonished to always look at the context the verse is in. While the word baptize is not in the passages, we must look to see if it was ever implied. Was Jesus talking about baptism in those passages?

> *And they brought unto Him also infants, that he would touch them: but when his disciples saw it, they rebuked them. But Jesus called them unto Him and*

said, "Suffer little children to come unto me, and forbid them not; for of such is the Kingdom of God. Verily I say unto you, whosoever shall not receive the Kingdom of God as a little child shall in no wise enter therein.

Luke 18:15-17

It is obvious in the passage that no baptizing was going on. People were bringing their children to Jesus, but they wanted Him to lay hands on the infants and *bless* them. This is what it says. To infer that Jesus was doing anything but what it says is not only incorrect but is bordering on blasphemy if the person knows the truth and is purposely misusing the Word of God.

For some reason the disciples didn't want babies to come around Jesus. It doesn't say why. But if baptism were necessary for the infants to avoid hell or to make them Christians, then one would think they would have been quick to baptize. The fact they rebuked the parents for coming tells us the disciples definitely weren't planning on baptizing the babies. When Jesus was a baby, He was never baptized. Luke chapter 2 speaks of His circumcision and when He was held and blessed. Jesus was dedicated in the temple. Many churches correctly do what Mary and Joseph did, bring the baby to the house of God and dedicate and bless the child. No water was added just to make sure all was done correctly.

Jesus was upset when the children were kept from Him. He scolded the disciples and commanded them to let the children come to Him; don't forbid it. The Kingdom of God is populated with people just like them. As a matter of fact, a person can't even enter the Kingdom unless he/she enters like a child. Now this is interesting, because in Jesus' mind the children were *already* acceptable in His eyes. For of such is the Kingdom of God. There are babies in heaven right now! If babies die, they come as they are, baptized or not! Jesus didn't say that they first must be baptized. Dear reader, you and I must come to Jesus like an infant, or we will never enter the Kingdom. Remember John 3? Jesus told Nicodemus that he must be born again. We must become like children and be born again to enter into Jesus' Kingdom. And Jesus didn't even mention baptism to Nicodemus. Surely if one entered the Kingdom from baptism, Jesus would have told Nicodemus. Jesus never told Nicodemus, His disciples, or the parents of the children that that was the case.

What *did* Jesus do?

And He took them up in his arms, put His hands upon them, and blessed them.

Mark 10:16

Reader, bring your infant child to church. Have your pastor put his hands on him/her and bless the child. Have your child dedicated. You need to put your hands on the child and bless the child also. This can and should be done often. As we shall see, baptizing the child in not only unbiblical, but can be a stumbling block in the future for that child. Millions of well-meaning people think they are going to heaven because they were baptized. Bring the children to Jesus-not the baptismal font! I repeat: the children are already acceptable to Jesus. When the child is capable of knowing of sin and its conse-quences, then he/she will be capable of knowing the need of a Savior. As an act of consecration, bless and dedicate the child to the Lord. Someday the child will make his/her own choice for Jesus because the Holy Spirit will be drawing the child to Himself.

Churches and well-meaning pastors can quote the above passages of Scripture from now until the Lord returns and it will never ever pertain to infant baptism any more that it does to Holy Communion, weddings, or funerals. Repeating error over and over again does not somehow make the error correct.

Chapter 6

THE HOLY GHOST AND THE BAPTISM OF JESUS-PART 1

❧

It can be confusing regarding the Holy Ghost's involvement with baptism even though the Holy Ghost was present in a very real sense in the baptism of Jesus. Let's see what the Bible has to say:

> Then cometh Jesus from Galilee to Jordan unto John, to be baptized of him. But John forbad him, saying, "I have need to be baptized of thee, and comest thou to me?" And Jesus answering said unto him, "Suffer (permit) it to be so now: for thus it becometh us to fulfil all righteousness." Then he suffered him.
>
> And Jesus, when he was baptized, went up straightway out of the water: and, lo, the heavens were opened unto him, and he saw the Spirit of God descending like a dove, and lighting upon him: And lo a voice from heaven, saying, "This is my beloved Son, in whom I am well pleased." Then was Jesus led up of the spirit into the wilderness to be tempted of the devil.
>
> *Matthew 3:13-4:1*

When studying the baptism of Jesus, it is important to notice what the baptism didn't do. There are those who say that baptism washes away original sin or sins. Jesus didn't have any sins. There are Christians that claim the baptism saves a person (1 Peter 3:21). Jesus didn't need saving; He was the Savior. Everyone else John the Baptist baptized repented and confessed their sins before the actual baptism. Jesus never did. His actual coming to John for baptism brought John to repentance. Why then was Jesus baptized?

A simple answer to the question is what Jesus said: *"Suffer (permit) it to be so now: for thus it becometh us to fulfil all righteousness."* More modern English would put it like this, "Do it because it is necessary to do everything right." The New Living Translation has Jesus saying, *"It must be done, because we must do everything that is right." (NLT)* To show His pleasure, the Father in heaven said, *"This is My beloved Son, in whom I am well pleased."* Obviously to do something correctly will bring the Father's good pleasure to bear on the situation, including baptism. As in everything, Jesus provides the example to follow.

We should come to baptism with our sins already gone in God's eyes. The baptism doesn't get rid of sins; we are to pray for forgiveness BEFORE we come to baptism. We are to be saved BEFORE we come to baptism. Our being baptized is following the command of Jesus. It is necessary to fulfil all righteousness. When I become a Christian my sins are totally forgiven. The Spirit of Jesus dwells within me. In a sense, God the Father sees me as He sees His Son: without sin. Realize Jesus never had sinned; realize I am the worst of sinners. But something happened at Calvary. Some call it the great exchange: Jesus took on Himself all my sins, and I took upon me all His righteousness. He died for me on the cross; and I live in righteousness here on earth! It doesn't sound fair but God declares it-so it is.

44

When you and I follow in Jesus' steps, believe me, the Father is well pleased also. Can you imagine the great God of the universe getting mad at us for trying to follow baptism like Jesus did? Would He get angry and say, "Hey, you are trying to do it like Jesus! You aren't supposed to do it that way!" Lord, help me be just like Jesus. I want to follow Him every way I can. Reader, we don't get in trouble by trying to be like Jesus. We get in trouble when we try **not** to be like Jesus.

The Bible teaches that baptism is a figure or a picture of salvation. It follows salvation and is an answer of a good conscience toward God.

> *The like figure whereunto even baptism doth also now save us (not the putting away of the filth of the flesh, but the answer of a good conscience toward God,) by the resurrection of Jesus Christ.*
>
> *1 Peter 3:21*

A close and honest look at the above Scripture in its context tells us that baptism does not put away sins (the filth of the flesh) and that it is the answer of the good conscience one gets when forgiven. When my conscience bothers me, it is the Holy Ghost telling me to confess my sins and get right with God. When I am forgiven, I then have a good conscience and baptism is my answer to that. I should only be baptized with a good conscience. Baptism is the figure of our salvation. It is the representation of our salvation, which comes from the resurrection of Jesus Christ. As a figure, it shows our salvation experience united to the death, burial, and resurrection of Jesus Christ.

> *Know ye not, that so many of us as were baptized into Jesus Christ were baptized into his death? Therefore we are buried with Him by baptism into*

45

death: that like as Christ was raised up from the dead by the glory of the Father, even so we also should walk in newness of life.

Romans 6:3,4

Baptism unites the believer to Jesus. We die "into His death." We are buried with Him by baptism, and then we are raised up from the dead. This glorifies the Father. We then should walk in this newness of life-which is the new birth. Baptism is a burial, not a sprinkling on a baby's head. That is why only believers were ever baptized in the Bible, and then by immersion. Yes, they were buried in the water (a figure or symbol of death) and then raised out of the water (a figure or symbol of the resurrection.) Try explaining that to an infant before sprinkling water on him/her. Sprinkling is not a burial. An infant cannot know the deep significance of Bible baptism. This shows why babies were not able in the New Testament times to understand what baptism is all about. They can't know today either.

John 4:1,2 states that:

Jesus made and baptized more disciples than John, though Jesus Himself baptized not, but his disciples (did- added by author).

Once again we see that Jesus first made disciples, then they were baptized. Jesus didn't baptize people first, and then teach them the faith. Why do many churches do it differently than Jesus did? Can you see why most people in church today are confused about salvation? "Don't worry about being born again. You were born again when you were baptized as an infant," many clergyman have exclaimed to their bewildered parishioners.

Well, Jesus knows how baptism is to be taught. Let us see how Paul taught the subject. Read 1 Corinthians 1:14-18

I thank God that I baptized none of you...For Christ sent me not to baptize, but to preach the gospel.... For the preaching of the cross is to them that perish foolishness; but unto us which are saved it is the power of God.

Paul was not against baptizing. He could see some problems that the Corinthian church was having with baptism, so he made sure it was clear that he emphasized the gospel, preaching the cross of Jesus Christ, which is the power of God. If it was baptism, which made Christians, Paul would have been first in line to baptize. Paul knew that baptism didn't save, and that once people believed, then they should be baptized.

In Acts 16, Paul and Silas were thrown in jail in Philippi for preaching the gospel and casting out demons. Not to let jail bars stop them, the two powerful Christians began to pray and sing aloud, other prisoners and guards hearing them. Suddenly an earthquake shook the foundations of the prison and Paul and Silas were loosed. The jailer was so scared and amazed, he cried out,

"Sirs, what must I do to be saved?"

Paul and Silas said in tandem,

"Believe on the Lord Jesus Christ and thou shalt be saved, and thy house."

Then the jailer took Paul and Silas to his home, where his whole family and possibly servants were preached to. Then the jailer's household was baptized, *believing in God with all his house (verse 34).*

We can learn three important lessons from this:

1. To become saved, one must believe on the Lord Jesus Christ.

2. When one person gets saved, his whole family is next in line.
3. Only believers can be baptized.

In closing the subject of baptismal regeneration (being born again by baptism,) let's make a generalization. Whether the Bible teaches to believe and be baptized (Mark 16:16), repent and be baptized (Acts 1:38), or to baptize after teaching disciples of all nations (Matthew 28:19), baptism ALWAYS follows belief. It never caused belief or came before belief. By putting it before belief, baptism can become an idol that people worship and think brings salvation and the Holy Spirit. That is why millions of people are heading for an eternal hell: trusting in a baptismal rite performed on them by a well-meaning pastor/priest.

Let us agree with Philip the evangelist. Baby baptizers should take a lesson from this New Testament saint. After he preached Jesus to the Ethiopian, the high official of Ethiopian monarchy said, *"See, here is water; what doth hinder me to be baptized?"* And Philip said, *"If thou believest with all thine heart, thou mayest."* *(Acts 8:36,37)* Philip was basically saying, "I will baptize you if you believe with all your heart. If you don't believe, I won't." After the Ethiopian confessed Jesus as the Son of God, they both went down into the water and Philip baptized the Ethiopian. This was pleasing to the Father and the Holy Ghost, who arranged the whole episode (Acts 8:26, 39.) Please note that had the Ethiopian not believed with his whole heart, Phillip would never have baptized him. Also they both went into the water. Philip didn't put a moist hand on the official's forehead and call it a baptism.

Baptism doesn't make Christians. Christians are supposed to be baptized. It is necessary to fulfil all righteousness. Believers are to be baptized in the Name of the Father, and of the Son, and of the Holy Ghost (Matthew 28:19). The Holy

Spirit of God declares it. *Let God be true, but every man a liar (Romans 3:4).*

Chapter 7

THE HOLY GHOST AND THE BAPTISM OF JESUS-PART 2

⌘

The last chapter dealt with the baptism of Jesus and compared it with some church practices of today. Jesus was never baptized as a baby. He never baptized a baby. John the Baptist never baptized a baby either. John did comment on what happened when Jesus was baptized.

"I saw the Spirit descending from heaven like a dove, and it abode upon him. And I knew him not: but he that sent me to baptize with water, the same said unto me, "Upon whom thou shalt see the spirit descending, and remaining on him, the same is he which baptizeth with the Holy Ghost. And I saw, and bare record that this is the Son of God."

John 1:32-34

The previous chapter had Matthew's account:

And Jesus, when he was baptized, went up straightway out of the water: and, lo, the heavens were opened unto him, and he saw the Spirit of God

51

*descending like a dove, and lighting upon him: And
lo a voice from heaven, saying, "This is my beloved
Son, in whom I am well pleased."*

Mat. 3:16,17

Here we see the totality of the Godhead. Jesus is baptized, the Holy Spirit comes upon Jesus, and the Father speaks. Is it any wonder then that Jesus would want Christians to be baptized in the name of all Three (the Trinity) as He said in Matthew 28:19? Cultists that deny the Triune nature of God will often baptize in a different mode or with a different verbiage than what Jesus commanded. They have to in order to skirt around what Jesus said, what the Holy Ghost inspired, and what pleased the Father. Dear reader, be baptized like Jesus said: not like some misinformed person may tell you. Be baptized *"in the name of the Father, and of the Son, and of the Holy Ghost"* as in the Gospel account.

Let's take a look at the role of the Holy Ghost in the baptism of Jesus. First of all, Jesus did not receive the indwelling of the Holy Spirit at His baptism. He was already God in human flesh. The Holy Spirit was always in Jesus while Jesus was on earth. Jesus was conceived by the Holy Spirit. Colossians 2:9 states,

*For in him dwelleth all the fullness of the Godhead
bodily.*

All the fullness of the Trinity dwells in Jesus, which includes the Holy Spirit. But in all the Bible passages which speak about the baptism of Jesus, it never says the Spirit came *into* Him, but always says the Spirit came *upon* Him. This is important and needs to be repeated: the Spirit came upon Jesus and not in Him. The baptism is recorded in all four Gospels. All four speak about the Spirit coming *upon* Jesus. What is the difference between the Holy Spirit coming upon or into someone? Is it important? And does it pertain to you and me?

Jesus spoke of a difference between the Holy Spirit being *in* someone and the Holy Spirit coming *upon* a person. When someone becomes a Christian, the Holy Spirit comes and lives *inside* the new creation. We sometimes say that Jesus lives inside the believer when we really mean the Spirit of Jesus lives inside. Jesus said in John 14:16-17:

> *"And I will pray the Father, and he shall give you another Comforter, that he may abide with you forever; Even the Spirit of truth; whom the world cannot receive, because it seeth him not, neither knoweth him: but ye know him; for he dwelleth with you, and shall be in you."*

Jesus was speaking to His disciples, who were not yet Christians. Jesus had not yet died for their sins, nor been resurrected. But He was letting them know ahead of time that the Holy Spirit was coming to be a Comforter to them, while actually living inside each believer. This indwelling Holy Spirit was to teach them and to bring to their memory all things Jesus had told them (John 14:26.) This explains why the Bible is such a perfect book, without error. The Holy Spirit had inspired the whole process of writing the book: from the memory to the teaching each writer had (2 Timothy 3:16-17). The Holy Spirit living in us today does the same thing: teaches us and brings Bible verses to our memory at the right time. We will talk more of the indwelling Spirit later. The point is: Jesus said that the Holy Spirit would live *in* believers.

After His resurrection, before returning to His Father, Jesus did a remarkable thing and actually gave the disciples the indwelling Spirit. Jesus said in John 20:21-22:

> *"Peace be unto you: as my Father hath sent me, even so send I you."* And when he had said this, he

breathed on them and saith unto them, "Receive ye the Holy Ghost."

Remember in Chapter 2 when we said that the word Spirit means breath or wind? Jesus actually breathed His breath on them, literally imparting His Spirit into the disciples. The resurrected life of Jesus was now placed into believers securing eternal life to those who received. Now these born-again believers would live forever, and even be able to forgive others their sins (John 20:23)!

I tell you these things to make the case that this was not what happened to Jesus at His baptism. Because at His baptism the Holy Ghost came *upon* Jesus and not *into* Him. *Upon* is not the same as *in*. The Holy Ghost *upon* you and I is not the same as the Holy Ghost *in* us either.

After Jesus gave the disciples the indwelling Spirit, He said something very important but often not taught in Christian circles. That was in Luke 24:49:

"And behold, I send the promise of my Father upon you: but tarry ye in the city of Jerusalem, until ye be endued with power from on high."

Then, just before He was taken up to heaven, Jesus repeated Himself. It was that important.

"But ye shall receive power, after that the Holy Ghost is come upon you: and you shall be witnesses unto me both in Jerusalem, and in all Judea, and in Samaria, and into the uttermost part of the earth."
                                                      Acts 1:8

Jesus told those who already had the indwelling Holy Ghost, to start their actual ministry *after* the Holy Ghost came *upon* them and gave them supernatural power. When did Jesus begin His public ministry? *After* the Holy Ghost came *upon* Him! Jesus waited with ministry till He was given Holy Ghost power to perform. Being God in the flesh, Jesus *could* have done miracles on His own. He wanted to serve not with His own desires and strength, but only that of His Father which made it necessary that He operate only with the Holy Spirit being *upon* Him. It was the correct thing to do. Jesus said that it was necessary to fulfill all righteousness (Mathew. 3:15).

It was after the Holy Spirit came *upon* Jesus that He had the anointing to accomplish great things for the Father. He didn't do it on His own power or authority, he waited till He was endued with power from on high. Why is that not taught for the most part in modern Christianity? The next question follows: why is there so little power in modern Christianity? Could it be that Jesus did it this way for our example, so that we would follow Him and get some of the same results He did? Or do you think we can get better results by doing things differently than Jesus did. What is the Holy Ghost telling you right now?

Chapter 8

THE ANOINTED SAVIOR

⤳

One of the things you may not have been taught is: what is a Christian? I thought I always knew what a Christian was. A Christian is a follower of Christ. This is a standard definition. Webster's New World Dictionary (2nd College Edition) defines a Christian as a person professing belief in Jesus as the Christ. This would be a good, partial definition if one knew what the word "Christ" meant. Ask the average Christian what the word Christ means and you see a funny expression come across his/her face. I have asked hundreds what the word Christ means, *very* rarely getting the correct answer.

Do you know what this means? The overwhelming majority of people who call themselves Christian has no idea what the word Christ means. How can someone be something he/she has no comprehension of what it is? Can you see the dilemma the Church of Jesus Christ is in? Can it be that the present Church of Jesus Christ has less apparent power than the early Church (seen in the book of Acts) because we are clueless as to who or what we are? Do you think the beginning Church had an idea of its identity? What does "Christ" mean and where did we "lose" it?

Let me first point out that Christ was not the last name of Jesus. He was not the son of Mary and Joseph Christ. We say the words "Jesus Christ" as if Jesus was His first name and Christ was His last. That is where we lose it. Jesus of Nazareth is the name given Him in the Bible and "The Christ" is the title and description given Him. Jesus is and was the Christ. He didn't come from the Christ family. The letters D.C. are behind my name. One of my degrees is Doctor of Chiropractic. That is a title conferred upon me, but that isn't my name. I come from the Warner family-not the Chiropractic family. Most Christians haven't a clue as to what His title means.

The New Testament was written in the ancient Greek language. Centuries later it was translated into other languages. This is when problems with word meanings crept into our understanding of theology. Certain words, which were very easy to understand in the original language, became difficult to understand in our language. The Greek word *baptizo* means to dip or immerse. Rather than to think of baptism as an immersion (a Latin word meaning to plunge or dip into), many Christian churches think baptism is dropping holy water on a baby's head. If we dropped the word baptism and used a word we know the meaning of, like immersion, then there would never be any debate as to the mode used in the Bible. John the Baptist would be known as John the Immerser. Nobody would question how John baptized. Nobody would question how Jesus or anyone else in the Bible was baptized. They were immersed.

This brings us to the question of the meaning of "Christ." Christ means anointing. Christ is the Greek word for anointing. The Christ means the anointing, or the anointed one. Jesus was anointed. Jesus was Christ. He was anointed (christed) with the Holy Ghost. The word "Jesus" actually means Savior, or Jehovah Saves. Therefore Jesus Christ actually means Anointed Savior.

> *How God anointed (christed) Jesus of Nazareth*
> *with the Holy Ghost and with power: who went about*
> *doing good, and healing all that were oppressed of*
> *the devil; for God was with him.*
>
> *Acts 10:38*

The word "christed" is not a word I have ever seen, but it gives the essence of what I wanted to point out. The meaning of anoint is to pour, smear, and/or rub on or into. We could accurately say that God the Father poured, smeared and rubbed the Holy Spirit onto Jesus. Jesus was baptized in the Jordan River; then the Holy Spirit came upon Him. John saw what looked like a dove come on Jesus. Jesus knew that He had just been anointed with the Holy Spirit and power. As a matter of fact, God poured and smeared and rubbed so much Holy Ghost into/onto Jesus that He was *filled* with the Holy Ghost.

> *And Jesus being full of the Holy Ghost returned*
> *from Jordan, and was led by the Spirit into the*
> *wilderness.*
>
> *Luke 4:1*

This allowed Jesus to resist temptation of the devil for 40 days. The man Jesus, filled with the Holy Ghost, could overcome the Evil One. You, dear reader can overcome Satan when you are anointed (filled) with the same Holy Spirit with which Jesus was anointed. Remember, this filling or anointing is different from the indwelling of the Holy Spirit.

> *And when the devil had ended all the tempta-*
> *tion, he departed from him for a season. And Jesus*
> *returned in the power of the Spirit into Galilee: and*
> *there went out a fame of him through all the region*

round about. And he taught in their synagogues, being glorified of all.

Luke 4:13-15

This is when Jesus began His earthly ministry. He did not start His ministry until he received power from the Holy Spirit. Timing was everything in Jesus' ministry. We send out ministers when they finish their education. They get a theological degree, but not necessarily the Holy Ghost. Is there any wonder why our churches are in trouble? And if our pastors don't have this anointing of the Holy Spirit, how can they teach those in the pews? They don't know what the word "Christ" means either! They can even know the Greek language and not have the Holy Ghost. Jesus didn't get the Holy Ghost when He learned Greek or graduated from school. After God anointed Jesus with the Holy Ghost and power (Acts 10:38), Jesus could stand in the synagogue and say:

"The Spirit of the Lord is upon me, because he hath anointed me to preach the gospel to the poor; he hath sent me to heal the broken-hearted, to preach deliverance to the captives, and recovering of sight to the blind, to set at liberty them that are bruised, to preach the acceptable year of the Lord."

Luke 4:18,19

Jesus said that the Spirit was *upon* Him. Jesus said that He was anointed (christed) to preach, heal and to free those bound by sin and disease. Do you see, dear brother/sister, that you certainly can't do any effective ministry without the anointing/filling of the Holy Ghost? You need the Spirit *upon* you with power.

Paul told the Corinthian Church:

> *Therefore If any man be in Christ (the Anointing,*
> *or Anointed One), he is a new creature; old things are*
> *passed away; behold, all things are become new.*
> *2 Corinthians 5:17*

If we are in the Anointing, we won't be the same. Something new awaits us. When we receive power, then we will be the witnesses Jesus spoke about in Acts 1:8. My friend, are you in Christ? Are you filled with the Holy Spirit? Are you really a Christian? Are you anointed?

If you want a theological education not taught or emphasized in most seminaries and Bible schools, read your New Testament with "anointing" substituted for "Christ." You will gain an understanding of scripture that was there all the time, but you had missed it. You just didn't know what "Christ" or "Christian" really meant.

Chapter 9

THE FRUIT OF THE SPIRIT

~⊗~

But the fruit of the Spirit is love, joy, peace, long-suffering, gentleness, goodness, faith, meekness, temperance: against such there is no law.

Galatians 5:22, 23

W hen the Holy Spirit comes into a person certain qualities are to be noted. These nine qualities listed above are evidence that the Holy Ghost is abiding or living in that person. This could also be called the characteristics of a Christian. Jesus had all nine fruit on display for our observance and example. The fruit of the Spirit are not to be confused with the gifts of the Spirit, which are dealt with in another chapter. Both fruit and gifts are needed. The fruit demonstrates who the person is and the gifts tell what the person does. This will clear up a lot of misunderstanding: the fruit shows who the person is while the gifts show what the person does.

First, let's look at the natural fruit found in the non-believer, or what we can call the fruit of the flesh. When you see the fruit of flesh, which the Bible calls the works of the flesh, one can easily spot a non-believer. This rotten fruit was never associated with Jesus.

This I say then, Walk in the Spirit, and ye shall not fulfill the lust of the flesh. For the flesh lusteth against the Spirit, and the Spirit against the flesh: and these are contrary the one to the other: so that ye cannot do the things that ye would. But if ye be led of the Spirit, ye are not under the law.

Now the works of the flesh are manifest, which are these; Adultery, fornication, uncleanness, lasciviousness, idolatry, witchcraft, hatred, variance, emulations, wrath, strife, seditions, heresies, envyings, murders, drunkenness, revellings, and such like: of the which I tell you before, as I have also told you in time past, that they which do such things shall not inherit the kingdom of God.

Galatians 5:16-21

The Word of God is very plain in this matter: people who exhibit these traits or fruit will not inherit the kingdom of God. Paul says in effect, "I told you this before, more than once, and I'm telling you now, Christians don't do these things. That is not what they are." This is stating a Bible truth. When we state this we are not judging someone. We need to state the plain facts and let the Word judge the listener.

Jesus said, "Judge not, that ye be not judged." (Matthew 7:1). He goes on to say that we will be judged the same way we judge others. I can't be the judge and tell you that you are going to hell. But I can state that if you are living in the lusts of the flesh, God says that such people are bound for hell. It is a fine line, but let the Word of God do the talking. People will then have to argue with God and not you. It will always work out better for them and us if we let God do the judging.

Quoting a Bible verse in love for another will do wonders in having the Holy Spirit bring conviction of sin to a lost soul.

Let me give a little illustration. A friend of mine and I went golfing one time and were paired with another two men. My friend and I were Christians, while I was unaware of the other two at first. One man was wearing a cap identifying a Catholic school, while the other, an excellent golfer, started swearing soon into the game. Now the swearing man was by far the best golfer of the foursome, but was never satisfied with his shots. "Jesus — — —" and "God — —" kept coming out of his mouth on practically every hole. He even threw his clubs once in awhile. I didn't know what to do or say, afraid he might get violent. I asked the Holy Spirit what I should do or say.

Luke 6:45 states, *"A good man out of the good treasure of his heart bringeth forth that which is good; and an evil man out of the evil treasure of his heart bringeth forth that which is evil: for of the abundance of the heart his mouth speaketh."* What this man was speaking was what was in his heart. Near the end of the game, the Holy Spirit told me what to do.

"Bill," I remarked, "You are a good Catholic."

"How do you know?" he asked.

"Well, I wasn't sure you were Catholic. But I did know you were very religious. You like to say "God" and "Jesus" so much, I knew you had to be more religious than me."

Things got real quiet. Not a word was spoken the rest of the game and the Name of the Lord was not taken in vain from then on. At the end of the game I was given an apology and the friend with the cap laughed and said, "Yea, he is a Catholic." He could have been of any faith. Bill obviously wasn't following the teachings of his church. The point I'm making is that the Holy Spirit will give you the words to say that can bring conviction of sin to those with bad fruit.

Jesus also said, *"By their fruits ye shall know them."* (Matthew 7:20). So we should not judge another, but we should recognize a non-believer. That will allow us to pray for the individual, but also to avoid getting entangled with their lifestyle. Jesus went to homes of sinners, but never to sin with the person. And He tells us to observe their lives, or check the fruit. He says in Matthew 7 that good trees bring good fruit, bad trees bring bad fruit. The bad trees are eventually torn down and burned in the fire. The good trees are pruned to give more and better fruit (John 15).

So the bad trees with the bad fruit are burned in fire, while the good trees and the good fruit are preserved and bless our God. *"Herein is my Father glorified, that ye bear much fruit; so shall ye be my disciples,"* Jesus said in John 15:8. His disciples will bear much fruit, and it will be good and God will get the glory, not us. We only bear good fruit because we are joined by the Holy Spirit to the vine. We can do nothing and display no good fruit without sticking to the vine. Jesus said that He was the vine, we are the branches, and Spiritual fruit will grow on these branches (John 15:5).

What then determines if there will be good fruit or bad fruit? The obvious answer is the presence of the Spirit of God. The fruit of the Spirit will be good and the fruit without the Spirit (the fleshly fruit) will be bad. We can also say that the fruit will be good or bad depending on the person. A person asking for the Holy Spirit will eventually bear the good fruit (Luke 11:13). A person refusing the Holy Ghost will bear the bad fruit. So we can also say it is up to the person to decide ultimately. God allows people to choose Him and the good fruit or the devil and the bad. There are Hyper-Calvinists who would argue that God decides and that the people have no say in the matter. It is up to God. But God said through Joshua very plainly, *"Choose you this day whom ye will serve" (Joshua 24:15)*. The good fruit depends on whether or not we are abiding in the vine.

One can also say that the kind of fruit depends on the seeds that have been planted. Plant good seeds and get good fruit. Plant the bad and get the bad or evil fruit. Luke 8:11 states that the good seed is the Word of God. By planting the good seed into your life you are assured a good harvest of fruit, even up to 100 fold! This is talked about in Matthew 13, Mark 4, and Luke 8. If you want a large harvest-you have to plant a lot of seed. Therefore, I can play a part also in getting a large harvest (or showing the fruit of the Spirit) by reading and studying my Bible. Lots of Bible, lots of fruit. Little Bible, little fruit. It is up to me. Faith comes by hearing the Word of God (Romans 10:17). My level of faith is up to the amount of hearing God's Word that I do. It is not up to God. He has already done His part in giving us His Word. He tells us to read/heed/hear/study His Word, and the results promised will come. He gives us His seed; it is up to us what we do with it. I certainly cannot blame God for the little fruit in my life! If we hear the Word with an honest and good heart, and obey what it says, we will bear the good fruit if we are only patient (Luke 8:15).

The fruit of the Spirit: love, joy, peace, longsuffering (patience), gentleness, goodness, faith, meekness, and temperance will be observed by yourself and others if the Holy Spirit abides in you. The Holy Spirit will not be in or fill you if the Word of God isn't in you. In Ephesians 5:18,19 the Word says, *"And be not drunk with wine, wherein is excess; but be filled with the Spirit; speaking to yourselves in psalms and hymns and spiritual songs, singing and making melody in your heart to the Lord."* This shows definite love, joy, peace, etc. But Colossians 3:14-16, says to put on love, peace, thankfulness, and to *"Let the word of Christ dwell in you richly in all wisdom; teaching and admonishing one another in psalms and hymns and spiritual songs, singing with grace in your hearts to the Lord."* It is up to you and I to put the seed of God's Word into us, so that the Holy Spirit has something to work with. Many times Christians fail in their walk because there is no Word in them to come out of them. Fill your heart with Bible passages, and when the time comes and you are in a fix, you will be able to reach within yourself and only the fruit of the Spirit will come out and be evident, because that is what is in there!

If you plant apple seeds, you will get apple trees. If you plant watermelon seeds, you won't get corn. Plant the seeds of love, joy, peace; and that is what you will get for fruit. *The amount and type of fruit you exhibit is determined by the amount and type of seed you plant into yourself.* If you pray for more fruit in your life, God will tell you to plant more seed.

Chapter 10

ARE ALL CHRISTIANS FILLED WITH THE HOLY SPIRIT?

No.

I want to be very emphatic about this. The answer is a definite "No." Just as the Church has often misinterpreted important meanings like baptism, somewhere we missed it concerning being filled with the Holy Ghost. The early Church knew exactly what being filled with the Holy Ghost was all about.

> *"And there appeared unto them cloven tongues like as of fire, and it sat upon each of them. And they were all filled with the Holy Ghost, and began to speak with other tongues, as the Spirit gave them utterance."*
>
> *Acts 2:3, 4*

In Acts 4:8 the filling is mentioned again:

"Then Peter, filled with the Holy Ghost, said unto them......"

Another place:

"And when they had prayed, the place was shaken where they were assembled together; and they were all filled with the Holy Ghost, and they spake the word of God with boldness."

Act 4:31

The book of Acts is often called the "Acts of the Apostles." But it would more accurately be called the "Acts of the Holy Spirit through the Apostles." I recently read the book of Acts and highlighted every word "Spirit" or "Ghost" I found and received a theological education! It is a Holy Spirit book and the early church knew it. The New Testament shows that individuals were at times filled and at times not filled.

Paul told the Ephesian Christians to "Be filled with the Spirit." (Ephesians 5:18). Obviously, some were not filled. That's why he told them to be filled. There were Christians in Ephesus not filled, just as there are Christians today not filled with the Spirit. There are whole denominations and churches ignoring the teaching on the filling of the Holy Ghost. Is there any wonder why the Church is so powerless compared to the Church of Acts? We don't even know that there is such a thing as filling or baptism of the Holy Spirit. Seminaries and Bible colleges that used to teach the topic are strangely quiet when someone mentions the filling/baptism. That is why many graduates now preaching in our churches have so little power and those sitting in the pews are clueless as to why.

The devil scored a major victory when the Church quit teaching on the filling or the baptism of the Holy Spirit. In the eighteenth and nineteenth centuries certain churches and preachers were teaching on the filling, but as the twentieth century progressed there was less and less of the topic, especially in mainline denominations. It took Pentecostal and Charismatic movements to restore what was commonplace in the original Church. Then comes a man like Bill Bright and Campus Crusade for Christ which put the "filling" back into Christian service. Campus Crusade has a wonderful pamphlet, *"Have You Made the Wonderful Discovery of the Spirit-Filled Life?"* This tract simply, yet powerfully, explains the filling for those new to the subject, without getting into speaking in tongues. I believe Mr. Bright wanted believers filled with the Holy Spirit and not have to deal with what is at times divisive in the Church.

Dwight Moody in the 1800s taught and wrote about the filling/baptism of the Holy Ghost. On page 17 of his book, *Secret Power* (Regal Books, publisher, copyright 1987), Dwight Moody states:

"I was crying all the time that God would fill me with His Spirit. Well, one day, in the city of New York-oh, what a day!-I cannot describe it, I seldom refer to it; it is almost too sacred an experience to name. Paul had an experience of which he never spoke for fourteen years. I can only say that God revealed Himself to me, and I had such an experience of His love that I had to ask Him to stay His hand. I went to preaching again. The sermons were not different; I did not present new truths, and yet hundreds were converted. I would not now be placed back where I was before that blessed experience if you should give me all the world-it would be as the small dust of the balance."

From that point on Dwight Moody turned the world upside down for Christ. He now preached with authority. Great crowds attended his services in Chicago and around the world. Millions ended up getting saved. His right hand man, R. A. Torrey, was the first president of Moody Bible Institute. Not only did Dwight Moody frequently ask Torrey to teach and preach on the filling or baptism of the Holy Spirit, but Torrey often refers to it in his books, one titled *The Baptism of the Holy Spirit*. His book is highly recommended by this author. The teaching and preaching of Spirit baptism was a part of on-fire Christianity in the late nineteenth century. This was the message of the greatest evangelistic movements in the United States. The period of time is not known for the number of babies that were baptized. It was Spiritual baptism. Much of the present Church of Jesus Christ is like the Church of Ephesus was before Paul came to visit in Acts 19.

> *Paul having passed through the upper coasts came to Ephesus; and finding certain disciples, he said unto them, "Have ye received the Holy Ghost since ye believed?" And they said unto him, "We have not so much as heard whether there be any Holy Ghost."*
>
> Acts 19:1,2

Then Paul taught them correctly, they were baptized correctly, and when Paul laid his hands on them, *"The Holy Ghost came on them; and they spake with tongues, and prophesied (verse 6).*

The key to this is when the Bible refers to the men Paul talked to as believers. *"And finding certain disciples,"* certainly would make them Christians. Paul then asks them, *"Have ye received the Holy Ghost since ye believed?"* There is no question about these men being believers or disciples. These people were like millions of church goers in this world, "We never even heard about this Holy Ghost. They don't teach us that in our church." These twelve men accepted the teaching of Paul, and received the filling of the Holy Spirit. They were not just Christians anymore; they were Spirit-filled Christians.

This baptism or filling with the Holy Ghost was taught throughout Paul's ministry. Even years later when Paul wrote to the Ephesian church, he was inspired to tell the Christians there again, *"Be filled with the Spirit (Ephesians 5:18).* Some of them, like some of us, needed to be filled.

The next question is an important one. Are you, dear reader, filled/baptized with the Holy Spirit? Do you want to be? I can remember the day when I decided I wanted the filling. I had been taught that speaking in tongues was of the devil, and I wanted nothing of it. But yet I decided to get the filling, and whatever came with it. I took off my religious hat and received the filling of the Spirit of God. I told God that I wanted whatever He wanted. Don't be afraid of the Holy Spirit. *"God hath not given us a spirit of fear; but of power, and of love, and of a sound mind." (2 Timothy 1:7)* You may or may not speak with tongues immediately after. I'm just asking the question, "Do you want to be filled?"

Let's take up the topic of tongues for just a moment. We will deal with it later in depth. The question we need to ask is: how did Luke know that people were filled with the Spirit when he wrote the book of Acts? Seeing that a person will look the same, filled or not filled, how did the writer of Acts know when someone was filled? The answer is that tongues were the evidence of this filling.

And they were all filled with the Holy Ghost, and began to speak with other tongues, as the Spirit gave them utterance.

Acts 2:4

These were all believing Jews who were filled or baptized with the Holy Spirit. Later Gentiles were also filled.

While Peter yet spake these words, the Holy Ghost fell on all them which heard the Word. And

they of the circumcision which believed were aston-
ished, as many as came with Peter, because that on
the Gentiles also was poured out the gift of the Holy
Ghost. For they heard them speak with tongues, and
magnify God.

Acts 10:44-46

Then, of course, the previously mentioned verse:

And when Paul had laid his hands upon them,
the Holy Ghost came on them; and they spake with
tongues, and prophesied.

Acts 19:6

Now, there are other evidences mentioned in the Acts. At times they were filled with joy and the Holy Ghost. Other times it states they were filled with the Spirit and spoke the Word of God boldly. One doesn't have to speak with tongues to be filled with the Spirit. But that being said, tongues was the evidence that others could recognize and it was the norm at least for the initial filling or first time filling/baptism of the Holy Ghost. In the Biblical instances when being filled has no specific mention of tongues, it is possible that tongues were present and just not mentioned. But whether tongues were present of not, we do know that most often they were mentioned.

For they heard them speak with tongues, and
magnify God.

Acts 10:46

One can and often is filled with joy when speaking tongues and the speaking of tongues can lead to boldness in speaking the Word in recognizable language. Therefore, tongues were probably always present with the Spirit baptism.

As previously state, the author was taught that tongues were of the devil, and that Spirit-filled tongues ceased when the Bible was written. Therefore I resisted speaking in tongues! I received the filling around the time of reading the Campus Crusade pamphlet and by faith "took it." Later on I learned more correctly the proper use of tongues from a Biblical standpoint, not a "religious" one. I now speak with tongues, but not around those people unfamiliar with it. It is not a 'badge" I wear or something to boast about to those who don't speak in tongues. Nevertheless, in the book of Acts speaking in tongues is the evidence of being filled/baptized with the Spirit, as it also is today. The important thing is not the speaking in tongues, but the receiving of POWER when the Spirit comes upon you. You will then be the witness God wants you to be. Are you open to it?

Chapter 11

DO ALL CHRISTIANS HAVE THE INDWELLING HOLY SPIRIT?

Y es. The Holy Spirit lives or dwells *inside* the Christian. If you are born again it is the life of Christ, or the Spirit of Christ, that is in your being. If you confessed your sins, repented, and received Jesus as your Savior, His Spirit came into you and you became a new creature. We covered this in Chapter One. The body of Jesus didn't enter in, but His Spirit did. Isn't this an awesome thought: the very Spirit of God dwells inside of you? He takes up residence in your body to give you new life, direct your thoughts, bringing His fruit with Him so that you will bear the fruit of the Spirit. He then will take you to the physical presence of God as soon as you die. Your old body will be left behind. No need of that: God has a new one in plan for you. He will never leave you nor forsake you (Hebrews 13:5). To be absent from the body is to be present with the Lord (2 Corinthians 5:8). It is the indwelling Holy Spirit that makes this possible.

Without the Holy Ghost dwelling within a person, he cannot be a Christian. The Word of God is very plain about this.

Now if any man have not the Spirit of Christ, he is none of his.

Romans 8:9b

This verse tells us directly that if someone does not have the Spirit of Jesus dwelling in him, he is not a Christian. *He is none of his.*

"Well, Brother Warner, what if the person is of another religion?"

"He is none of His," I reply.

"I have a friend who likes to talk about God. Just because my friend doesn't have the Holy Ghost, surely doesn't mean he is lost and going to hell."

"He is none of His," again I say.

"But you don't know about this person's sincerity! He believes in God. He goes to church every week. He's a great guy! God won't keep this man out of heaven."

"He is none of His," I reply. If any person doesn't have the Spirit of Christ living in him, he is not a part of the body of Christ. I don't like to be the bearer of this kind of news, but I am only repeating what Paul said under the inspiration of the Holy Ghost. If the Spirit says it is so, who are we to argue?

And if Christ be in you, the body is dead because of sin; but the Spirit is life because of righteousness. But if the Spirit of him that raised up Jesus from the dead dwell in you, he that raised up Christ from the dead shall also quicken your mortal bodies by his Spirit that dwelleth in you.

Romans 8:10, 11

For as many as are led by the Spirit of God, they are the sons of God.

Romans 8:14

The sons of God (Christians) are led by the Holy Spirit that dwells in them and gives them life. This life is living in a temple, which is your body if you are a Christian.

> *What? Know ye not that your body is the temple of the Holy Ghost which is in you, which ye have of God, and ye are not your own?*
> *For ye are bought with a price: Therefore glorify God in your body, and in your spirit, which are God's.*
>
> *1 Corinthians 6:19,20*

Paul, writing to the Corinthian Christians, told them to glorify God in their bodies and spirits, which were bought with a great price: the very blood of Jesus. We are to do the same. Is God glorified in your body? Is your temple of the Holy Ghost polluted with cigarettes, alcohol, and poor nutrition? Is your temple fitting for the God of the universe to live in, or is it overweight and ready to collapse? How physically fit are you? Will your body present God to others? When people look at you, what do they see? True, God is inside of you. But people see the *outside* when they look at us. Some may never see the inside because the outside is so unappealing. Proper dress for Christians is in order. How do you drape the temple of God? Does it honor your Lord? Can people see that?

Before Jesus came and lived upon the earth, the Holy Spirit had not been sent to live within people. The Bible does a couple times refer to the Spirit inside of some before Jesus, but the Comforter was not sent to dwell in believers till Jesus rose from the dead.

> *And I will pray the Father, and he shall give you another Comforter, that he may abide with you forever;*

> *Even the Spirit of truth; whom the world cannot receive, because it seeth him not, neither knoweth him: but ye know him; for he dwelleth with you, and shall be in you*
>
> *John 14:16,17.*

It is this Holy Spirit living in the believer that guides us to truth, tells us the things of God, and shows us things to come(John 16: 13, 14). He reproves(or convicts) the world of sin, of righteousness, and judgment(John 16:8). God has chosen to use the body of you, dear believer, to live in and to work toward saving the lost souls of the world. That is the way God operates. He doesn't send angels to witness to the lost; He uses you and me. The angels are there to help, but God is inside to do the job!

Think of it this way. A room is empty. It could be your church building or any building. The Spirit of God is not present. When the first Christian walks into the room, the Holy Ghost walks in. Something has changed. A presence is there which wasn't there before. It doesn't matter how difficult a challenge or conflict may be, there is now the Holy Spirit getting involved. There is great confidence to a believer when he/she has the realization that the Holy Spirit is now walking into any circumstance or situation. Jesus said, "I will not leave you comfortless. The Holy Spirit within you will tell you what to say, when to say it, and what action to take (Warner paraphrase, Luke 12:11,12)." You will never more be alone. Your life will be totally different. Only the believer can witness this presence of the Holy Spirit.

> *The Spirit itself beareth witness with our spirit, that we are the children of God.*
>
> *Romans 8: 16*

All Christians have the indwelling Holy Spirit. But not all have the *filling* of the Holy Spirit, as our previous chapter explained. All Christians are going to heaven, whether filled or not. If you die half full you will still get there! He said He would never leave you or me. It is the Spirit that raised Christ from the dead that is living in the believer that will raise him/her up also.

There are Christians of various persuasions who don't believe in the baptism of the Holy Ghost. Some may think that those that do believe in the baptism think they are a "special breed" of Christian. Spirit-filled Christians sometimes may mistakenly say something that may be construed as such. People have a tendency not to understand something they have not experienced. Those of us who have experienced Spirit-baptism must be sensitive to the feelings of others. The next chapter will discuss how the Holy Ghost can come upon a person and he/she will be able to do things she couldn't do as a non-filled Christian. She may be an "ordinary" Christian, but an extraordinary God can fill her to overflowing and the gifts of the Spirit will become evident, as this Christian becomes much more effective in her service. It is not a "special breed" of Christian, but a special breed of God using this person in a powerful way.

Chapter 12

THE HOLY SPIRIT COMES
UPON PEOPLE

There is a big difference between the Holy Spirit coming upon someone and the Holy Spirit dwelling in someone. Many well-meaning Christians don't know the difference. To make it simple: the Holy Spirit dwells in the person who becomes a Christian. The Holy Spirit coming upon someone is a totally different experience that has not always happened to Christians. Someone may be a Christian and not have the Holy Spirit come upon them, and yet Jesus said that the experience is for the Christian to experience. Yet in the Old Testament the Holy Spirit came upon people who weren't spiritual by our thinking. Put another way: the Holy Ghost will come upon the Christian with the Christian's cooperation, but came upon people in the Old Testament at times without their cooperation. The Holy Spirit may at times come upon non-Christian people these days, but I am not aware if a good Bible case to support this is in existence. But if He came upon uncooperative people at one time, He can do it again at another time.

Let's look at a couple of Old Testament people who were not godly men by our thinking, yet the Holy Ghost came upon them powerfully. The first example I will discuss is Samson. We can find the readings in Judges 13-16. What a disappointment for God Samson was! Even his parents were upset with him. We are all impressed with Samson's physical strength, but not his moral strength.

Samson's parents raised him up to be a Nazarite. Nazarites were men who were separated unto God for a period of time, but Samson was to be a Nazarite from birth to death. This meant that he was to be different from others: no drinking of alcoholic beverages, a special diet, and a head of hair which would never be cut. So strict was this that he wasn't even to eat grapes, to make sure there was no fermentation, which is a form of corruption, to come to his lips. Numbers 6 gives a complete accounting of the Nazarite vow. The interesting thing about this and Samson is the hair. The long hair and special diet made the Nazarite "different" from others, as they were visibly to be separated for God's service. John the Baptist was a Nazarite. He had long hair, ate a special diet, and wore weird clothes. He was separated for God's service, a "voice of one crying in the wilderness." This was a special walk, one that John the Baptist successfully walked while Samson didn't.

The long hair of Samson was a symbol of the Holy Spirit covering the man. The Bible often uses symbols to represent the real thing. Jesus took bread and wine and said that these elements were to be a memorial, something to represent His body and blood. They are symbols of the very body and blood of Jesus. Samson's hair was a symbol of the covering of the Holy Ghost on his life. God was willing to "come upon" Samson and use him mightily as long as Samson revered this holy covering. When Samson lost his covering, the Holy Ghost left him and he was on his own. How important symbols can be! Just because people have the symbols, doesn't mean they have the real thing. But if you have the real thing, the symbol will usually be there.

*So the woman bore a son and called his name
Samson; and the child grew, and the Lord blessed
him. And the Spirit of the Lord began to move upon
him at Mahaneh Dan between Zorah and Eshtaol.*
Judges 13:24, 25 NKJV

Notice that the Spirit moved *upon* Samson and not *in*
him. The Holy Ghost was not abiding in Samson, but God
was able to move upon Samson and still accomplish God's
purposes. This was the source of his strength. Samson was
strong because the Holy Ghost was strong upon him, not just
because he missed a couple haircuts! The hair symbolized
the Holy Ghost. This is very important.

Young Samson was confronted by a lion:

*And the Spirit of the Lord came mightily upon
him, and he tore the lion apart....*
Judges 14:6 NKJV

It was the Holy Spirit that gave him his strength, when
the Spirit came *upon* him. Later on, the Holy Spirit came
upon Samson and he killed 30 evil men (Judges 14:19). Then
the Holy Spirit came upon him and he killed 1000 Philistines
with a jawbone of an ass (Judges 15:15)! Very few people
have been killed with a donkey's jawbone since. One didn't
mess with Samson.

But Samson had a weakness: women. We know he spent
the nights with at least one prostitute, and Delilah wasn't his
wife. Samson also was not respectful of his parents, was a
liar, and like Esau, was willing to give away his birthright
for short-term satisfaction. When Samson showed no respect
for God's symbol, Delilah was more than happy to take it
from him. When Delilah and an accomplice shaved his head,
Samson became weak like any other man (verse 16:17).

Samson knew that would happen. And it did happen because the Lord left when the covering left (verse 16:21).

Samson is a good illustration of the Lord "coming upon" someone even though the person wasn't a Christian, or had the Spirit living inside of him. Another good example is King Saul. King Saul was also a wicked king. He had his good points, but was found unfaithful, trying to kill David, offering profaned sacrifices, and on and on. Yet there were times when the Holy Spirit came upon him even though the Spirit didn't abide in him. Saul was anointed king by Samuel, who poured oil on his head, symbolizing the Holy Spirit's anointing on Saul (1 Samuel 10:1). The Spirit then came upon Saul (1 Samuel 10:6, 10:10, and 11:6) and he prophesied. When the Spirit departed from Saul (1 Samuel 16:14) he lost any special ability he had from God.

One can look at many other instances of the Holy Ghost coming upon people. The point I am making is that when the Holy Spirit comes upon someone, that person can then do things he would not be able to do without Him. Without the Spirit's power Samson, King Saul, and King David were mere men. But with the anointing of the Holy Ghost, nothing was impossible. Now if this is true, and I believe I have made a strong case, why is it that Christians would not know about this, or worse, would refuse it when told about it?

Another lesson can be learned from Moses, who lived 1400 years before Jesus came. Moses was Hebrew, not a born again Christian. The Holy Spirit had not been sent to dwell within. Yet we know the Holy Spirit came *upon* Moses. How else could he have performed all the miracles? The Bible even describes a "little Pentecost" occurring in the Old Testament.

Then the Lord came down in the cloud, and spoke to him, and took of the Spirit that was upon him, and placed the same upon the seventy elders; and

it happened, when the Spirit rested upon them, that
they prophesied, although they never did so again.
Numbers 11:25 NKJV

Isn't this interesting? The Spirit came upon seventy
Hebrew elders at the same time. How did people know that
the Spirit came upon them? They knew it because the seventy
prophesied, which meant they probably were speaking in
tongues. As discussed in a another chapter, tongues and
prophesying are the same thing in the New Testament, the
difference being prophesying is in a known language, while
tongues in an unknown. In the Old Testament when people
start prophesying, the meaning is usually with tongues. They
usually fell down on the ground when it happened. This was
not a very distinguished happening, and Joshua, like many in
our churches, got very upset.

"Moses my Lord, forbid them!"
Numbers 11:28b NKJV

But Moses, under the inspiration of the Holy Spirit,
spoke 1 Corinthians 14:29 centuries before Paul did.

Then Moses said to him, "Are you zealous for my
sake? Oh, that all the Lord's people were prophets
and that the Lord would put His Spirit upon them!"
Numbers 11:29 NKJV

It was the desire of Moses and our God that *all* the Lord's
people would have the Holy Spirit come upon them, and all
would prophesy. Here we are, 3500 years later, and the issue
still isn't settled in our churches. We have people in churches
today that would run to Moses (or their pastor) even now and
say, "Forbid them!" just like Joshua did. Men like Moses and
St. Paul wouldn't last long in today's "Christian" churches.

Chapter 13

THE HOLY SPIRIT COMES
UPON CHRISTIANS

᠃᠊᠊᠊᠊᠊᠊᠊᠊

In a previous chapter, the case was made that Jesus had the Holy Ghost come *upon* Him, that the Holy Ghost *anointed* Him, and that the Holy Ghost *filled* Him. These terms are used pretty much interchangeably. In other places in the Bible we can add the baptism of the Holy Ghost along with receiving the Holy Ghost to these terms, but more accurately we would say one received the filling or baptism of the Holy Spirit. As had been discussed, this experience is different from becoming saved and having the Spirit live inside oneself. When the Holy Ghost lives inside someone, then they should exhibit certain fruit since the Holy Ghost is directing their lives. The Holy Spirit may direct their lives, but it is possible that the activities the saved person does may not exhibit the *power* of the Holy Spirit. That person may be a wonderful neighbor to have; a person we would say is an ideal person. They are honest, upright, helpful, loving, church going people. But Holy Ghost *power* to accomplish soul winning, witnessing, and exercising the gifts of the Spirit may be absent. Jesus spoke about this power:

In that last day, that great day of the feast, Jesus stood and cried, saying, "If any man thirst, let him come unto me, and drink. He that believeth on me, as the scripture hath said, out of his belly shall flow rivers of living water." But this spake he of the Spirit, which they that believe on him should receive: for the Holy Ghost was not yet given; because that Jesus was not yet glorified.

John 7: 37-39

To paraphrase this, Jesus was saying that if anyone was thirsty for the things of God, that person could be filled by coming to Jesus. Out of that person's belly or heart would flow rivers of living water. It is like a pipeline from God going into the person and flowing out of the person like a river, which signifies that person's service to others. There will be more than enough to satisfy the person and those to whom the flowing water goes. That person is a reservoir of living water to a dying world, filling up and flowing out. Jesus was speaking of a future event of the Spirit that *"they that believe on him should receive."* Notice Jesus is talking about believers, and that they *should* receive the Holy Ghost. That is something believers should receive. That should be the normal, and not the unusual.

In fairness, there are modern Bible versions that say the believers *would* receive. This is not the same as *should* like the King James Version says, but even the new translations acknowledge that one first believes and then receives the Holy Ghost with this passage. The point is that there can be a period of time from when one believes till one receives the power of the Holy Ghost.

Jesus teaches this principle again in the first chapter of Acts:

"For John truly baptized with water; but ye shall be baptized with the Holy Ghost not many days hence."

Acts 1:5

The question needs to be asked: was Jesus talking to believers? Of course He was. They were with the resurrected Christ. They believed he was risen and ready to leave earth. They also were not baptized (or filled, or anointed) with the Holy Ghost because Jesus said that they would be in a few days. They were believers, had been baptized in water, and yet were not filled with the Holy Ghost. Then Jesus said something else that was incredible and rarely seen today:

"But ye shall receive power, after that the Holy Ghost is come upon you: and ye shall be witnesses unto me both in Jerusalem, and in all Judaea, and in Samaria, and unto the uttermost part of the earth."

Acts 1:8

Here Jesus called the experience having the Holy Ghost come *upon* the believer; the previous sentence called it Holy Ghost baptism. In both cases the audience was the same: believers who had already received the indwelling Holy Ghost. Remember John 20:22, when Jesus breathed on them and said to receive the Holy Ghost? Now, days later He is telling them that they would receive power when the Holy Ghost comes *upon* them. At the time of Him saying that, they were Christians without the Holy Ghost power, much like millions of Christians today. Imagine that; the final words of our Savior falling on deaf ears! Where is the power?

Remember last chapter, when the Spirit came upon Samson and King Saul: how they were empowered to do things they otherwise couldn't do. It is the same with the Christian. When the Holy Ghost comes upon the believer, he or she receives power to do the things he/she couldn't otherwise do, Without the Spirit coming upon me (or baptizing me) I can still be a "good" Christian. But if I want **power** for service, I am going to have to have the Spirit anoint me, baptize me, fill me, and or come upon me! This is not emphasized in most Christian circles. That is why studies show that 95-98% of Christians have never led another person to Christ. Imagine that: a believing Christian who doesn't want anyone to go to hell will probably never powerfully witness to another person-never!

Friend, that is why this book is being written. If you want, you can receive this power that Jesus was talking about. It is the power to witness to a fallen world and win many to Christ. You will be part of the 2-5% to bring someone with you. Why not bring hundreds to heaven? Why can't this Biblical truth be accepted and proclaimed throughout the earth? If all Christians would win just one person, the whole world would be won for the Lord. But we will never do this without the power of the Holy Ghost. Don't bother to even try. Do it the Lord's way, and not your way.

Chapter 14

RECEIVING THE BAPTISM OF THE HOLY GHOST

⤙⤚

At this point in the book it is time to receive the baptism of the Holy Spirit. The case has been adequately made and one would really have to be "hard-boiled" to want to refuse this gift from God. I will deal with refusal in a later chapter. For now, to every doubter, I proclaim the words of the martyr Stephen:

> *Ye stiffnecked and uncircumcised in heart and ears, ye do always resist the Holy Ghost: as your fathers did, so do ye.*
>
> *Acts 7:51*

Don't resist the Holy Ghost, even if your family has up to now. I don't care what your denomination or church teaches. Pastor, will you refuse God's power for a denominational creed? Remember, even Moses wants all of God's people to have the Holy Spirit come upon them! Would you say "No" to Moses? Would you be offended at Paul wanting to lay his hands on you to receive the Holy Ghost? Will you tell Jesus that you don't want anything to do with Acts 1:8?

The twelve men in Ephesus (Acts 19) didn't have to read a whole book to make the decision. They accepted the Word of God as spoken by Paul and received the Holy Ghost right away. They didn't argue or tell Paul that the experience happened at Pentecost and wasn't for their day. They were honest men who wanted all God wanted to give them. They weren't more "holy" than other Christians and they didn't become more "holy" after they received. They just became more useful and effective.

R.A. Torrey said it well: "The baptism with the Spirit is not primarily intended to make believers happy nor holy, but to make them useful."

(Quotation coming from *What The Bible Teaches*, by R.A. Torrey, Fleming H. Revell Company, 1898-1933.)

There are basically only three steps to receive the baptism of the Holy Ghost. They are very simple, but have confounded Christians for centuries. They are:

1. Obedience
2. Asking
3. Receiving

Obedience

Without obedience the other two steps will not work. Many people have tried asking and receiving at the altar of churches but didn't precede with obedience. They might get excited, jump up and down, get "slain" in the spirit and fall on the ground and have resisted the first and most important step. I am not against getting excited. Receiving the Holy Spirit upon one's life is exciting! But to shout loudly and manufacture an "experience" that comes without obedience is shallow and won't last the next time the devil comes at you. In the Old Testament the Lord declares that He desires obedience more than any sacrifice.

By obedience I mean first of all to become a Christian. Chapter One dealt with becoming born again. Are you born again? Reread the chapter. Pray the prayer, meaning every word. You will then become born again and qualify to be filled with the Spirit of God.

A key part of the prayer was confession of sin. This is being obedient. If you don't confess your sins to God and man, you will never receive the Holy Spirit. I don't care how many churches you join or times you have been water-baptized. You know you are a sinner. So why don't you just confess it? God knows you are a sinner also. When you confess your sins is not when God first learns about it. That is when you get it off your chest and He takes it from you.

A Christian can have unconfessed sins also. They may even say a prayer, "Forgive me my sins, Lord." But God wants us to spell it out. One of the best things I ever did was to take a couple sheets of paper and write down *everything* I could think of from years gone by that I had sinned and grieved God with. This included the time before and after I was a Christian. What a long list I had! Then I prayed asking for God to forgive me for each one. It took awhile, but it was worth it. Then I destroyed the sheets of paper. Boy, did I feel free! Days later I remembered other things to pray for. God won't send you to hell for not remembering a sin. Otherwise we would all go to hell! But He does want us to confess our sins to receive forgiveness. Not forgiving others of their sins results in God not forgiving us ours (Matthew 6:15). Part of obedience is forgiving others of their sins.

Right along side confession is repentance. Every person on the street will confess they are a sinner. "Nobody is perfect." is a common saying. How many will repent? To repent means:

Repent: feel sorry for what one has done or failed to do, to feel such regret or dissatisfaction over some past action, intention, etc. as to change one's mind about, to feel so contrite over one's sins as to change....

From Webster's New World Dictionary (2nd College Edition)

So by definition to repent is to be so sorry for something that you will change the behavior. If you are living with a person of the opposite sex, you will either split up the unholy alliance or marry the person and make it right. If drunkenness is your sin, you will stop drinking. Now this may take time to leave a sinful lifestyle. But the choice to do so must be made and assistance looked for to help. Be willing to give up the sin, ask the Holy Ghost to come in, and He will give you the strength to overcome the sin. Don't wait till you are perfect to pray; pray now, get right with the Lord, and He will get you out of the lifestyle. You won't be able to without Him. Trying to stop drugs without the Lord is foolish. It can't be done. I have seen many people in jail get off drugs while incarcerated. But as soon as they get out......you know the story. But I have also seen the drug addict pray to confess and repent and be saved-and then able to resist the drugs-sometimes immediately.

Obedience also involves reading and knowing what God wants you to do and then doing it. It might not be a sinful lifestyle; it may just be following Jesus in what He wants. He wants you to be filled with His Spirit. Don't fight it-obey!

And we are his witnesses of these things; and so is also the Holy Ghost, whom God hath given to them that obey him.

Acts 5:32

Peter on that great day of Pentecost, after the crowd asked, "What shall we do?" told them to obey:

> *Then Peter said unto them, Repent, and be*
> *baptized every one of you in the name of Jesus Christ*
> *for the remission of sins, and ye shall receive the gift*
> *of the Holy Ghost.*
>
> *Acts 2:38*

Peter told them to repent and be baptized. If I wanted to be filled with the Holy Ghost, I would want to obey what Peter said. I would not resist repenting and being baptized. There is a biblical precedent to follow.

Usually the disciples would baptize before the new believer would receive the baptism of the Holy Ghost. Remember Paul at Ephesus?

> *When they heard this, they were baptized in the*
> *name of the Lord Jesus. And when Paul had laid*
> *hands on them, the Holy Spirit came upon them, and*
> *they spoke with tongues and prophesied.*
>
> *Acts 19:5, 6 NKJV*

In Acts 2:38 Peter taught the same thing: repent, be baptized, and receive the Holy Ghost. In Acts 8:14-17, Peter and John went to Samaria after they heard that the Samaritans had believed and had been baptized. They then laid hands on those Samaritans and they also received the Holy Ghost. This was the normal sequence of events. But God is not limited always to a particular sequence.

> *While Peter was still speaking these words, the*
> *Holy Spirit fell upon all those who heard the word.*
> *And those of the circumcision who believed were*
> *astonished, as many as came with Peter, because the*
> *gift of the Holy Spirit had been poured out on the*
> *Gentiles also.*

For they heard them speak with tongues and magnify God. Then Peter answered,

"Can anyone forbid water, that these should not be baptized who have received the Holy Spirit just as we have?"

And he commanded them to be baptized in the name of the Lord. Then they asked him to stay a few days.

Acts 10:44-48 NKJV

Notice that the Spirit baptism came *before* the water baptism. God knew the hearts of these Gentile converts and poured out His Spirit upon them. This astonished the Jewish believers for two reasons: that salvation came to the Gentiles and that the Spirit came upon them before they were baptized. They knew that the Gentiles were saved and filled with the Spirit because of the tongues and the praising of God. There was evidence that something occurred. Being obedient, the new converts were baptized in water.

My dear reader, don't wait to be filled with the Holy Ghost. If you have confessed your sins, repented, and will yet follow in baptism, the Lord may yet baptize you with His Spirit beforehand. But don't wait to be baptized in water any longer than you have to.

ASK

The second step in being baptized in the Holy Ghost is just to ask.

"If you then, being evil, know how to give good gifts to your children, how much more will your heavenly Father give the Holy Spirit to those who ask Him!"

Luke 11:13 NKJV

This is a marvelous verse of Scripture that shows how easy it is to get the Holy Spirit! It is simple but so profound, that like entering the straight and narrow gate, *few there be that find it!* Dear reader, if you have repented of your sins, are a Christian, and set your sights on being filled with the Holy Ghost, all you have to do is ask Him! *How much more* does your heavenly Father want you to have this anointing! Ask!

RECEIVING

The third and final step in obtaining the baptism of the Holy Spirit is to receive it. This works hand in hand with asking. Receiving is basically asking in faith.

> *But let him ask in faith, nothing wavering. For he that wavereth is like a wave of the sea driven with the wind and tossed.*
> *For let not that man think that he shall receive anything of the Lord.*
> *A double minded man is unstable in all his ways.*
> *James 1:6-8*

One has to ask in faith, not doubting that God will answer the prayer. Don't waver or question God on this. The whole book and every Scripture points out that God's will is to have this gift of the Holy Ghost. If God declares it-dear Christian just believe it. If you mean it when you ask, believe God that He wants to give the Holy Ghost baptism to you, just say "Yes, I receive it." Now it is final. You will have the filling of the Holy Spirit. Jesus said,

"Therefore I say to you, whatever things you ask when you pray, believe that you receive them, and you will have them."

> *Mark 11:24 NKJV*

When you finish this chapter, I want you to go to a quiet place, your prayer closet if you will, and pray to receive the Holy Spirit. Then consider it done. You will now have it. This is on the authority of the Word of God. You have fulfilled all requirements, and God declares it.

When the reality hits you, a joy unspeakable will set in. I don't know if it will be immediate, or minutes to hours later. But something will happen and you will *know* it. A warmth may set in, Goosebumps may go up and down your spine, you may fall to the floor, and tongues may be spoken. This will not be God forcing anything on you. You will be a willing participant. Your first attempt at tongues will sound goofy and you may feel weird. I tell people if that is the case you are probably doing it correctly! You won't understand it, but God will. You will be speaking mysteries (1Corinthians 14:2). If any non-filled person hears you, they will say you are nuts (1 Corinthians 14:23)! That's why you do it in private, unless you have a friend who is seeking the same as you. Then pray together. If the two of you agree upon this, you will have it! This is another Bible promise (Matthew 18:19).

If another believer is with you, have him/her lay hands on you, especially if that person is already Spirit filled. This frequently was the way the Spirit fell on people, though not always. I think that it is easy for the Spirit to flow from one person to another by way of touch (Acts 8:17). Jesus said that from your heart (belly) shall flow rivers of living water (Spirit). This can be from one Spirit-filled believer to the one desiring the filling. When the woman with the issue of blood touched Jesus, He felt virtue (power) leave Him and go to her. I believe it was the power of the Holy Ghost.

And when Paul had laid hands on them, the Holy Spirit came upon them, and they spoke with tongues and prophesied.   *Acts 19:6 NKJV*

A good confession to make when the Christian lays his/her hands on you, is "When Joe lays his hands on me, the Holy Spirit will come upon me." I would repeat this saying until satisfied I believe it. Faith comes by hearing the Word of God. Say it, believe it, receive it.

Enjoy this new sensation. Have an emotional high. It comes with the Spirit! But remember why you are experiencing this new encounter with God. It is to receive power to witness, utilizing the Spiritual gifts given you. This power with the gifts allows you to minister to others with great effectiveness. Remember what Torrey said, that this baptism is not primarily to make you happy nor holy, but to make you useful. But it is normal when filled to speak and sing in tongues with psalms, hymns, spiritual songs, and to make melody in your heart (Ephesians 5:18-19). God wants you to speak in tongues and to prophecy (1 Corinthians 14:5). To forbid the speaking in tongues for you or others is sin (1Corinthians 14:39).

Chapter 15

GREAT MOVEMENTS OF THE HOLY SPIRIT

⤞

From the first Pentecostal experience in Acts, chapter 2, till the present day, there has been great movements of the Holy Spirit. Any time that God moves to bless someone, it is a great thing for that person. Each of us can testify how God's Spirit moved in a particular way to bring us victory in various areas of our lives. When you and I, dear reader, received Jesus as our Lord and Savior, it was a great movement for us! God will bless each of us individually, but there are times when the individual blessing is multiplied thousands of times over. Jesus said that greater works than what He did, we would do, because He went to His Father and sent the Holy Spirit (John 14:12-17). Without the Spirit we can't do any great works, but with the Spirit in and upon us we can do the greater works Jesus was talking about. The Holy Spirit is the great adder and multiplier.

Jesus said:

> *...but wait for the promise of the Father, which, saith He, ye have heard of me. For John truly baptized*

with water; but ye shall be baptized with the Holy Ghost not many days hence.

Acts 1:4,5

Jesus told the disciples to wait till they were baptized with the Holy Ghost, and that they would then receive POWER to witness (verse 8). This happened on the day of Pentecost. Acts chapter 2 begins with 120 believers praying together in one accord. This means they were in agreement prayer as outlined in Matthew 18:19. They were praying for it to come to pass what Jesus said in Acts chapter 1, regarding the baptism of the Holy Ghost. Then it happened!

And suddenly there came a sound from heaven as of a rushing mighty wind, and it filled all the house where they were sitting. And there appeared unto them cloven tongues like as of fire, and it sat upon each of them. And they were all filled with the Holy Ghost, and began to speak with other tongues, as the Spirit gave them utterance.

Acts 2:2-4

This miracle drew quite a crowd, and with Peter's inspired preaching a great movement of God was to happen:

Then they that gladly received his word were baptized: and the same day there were added unto them about three thousand souls.

Acts 2:41

As noted above, each person who receives Jesus can claim a miracle for themselves. But when a great movement occurs, that miracle is multiplied in huge numbers, three thousand in first century Jerusalem that day: not an average day for Jerusalem.

An interesting side note is that in great movements of God not everyone will take part. Some will observe what is happening and come up with an excuse as to why it won't work for them. In effect, they refuse to receive God's Word that is being offered to the masses. We see this in verse 41, where it states; *"Then they that gladly received his word were baptized.."* Those that didn't receive were not baptized and were not a part of the three thousand. Some people today refuse to accept God's miracle power and nothing happens. They say, "This is just a bunch of baloney," or "That only happened at Pentecost and doesn't work any more." To them it is true. They will not see the great movements of the Holy Ghost. Those that believe and those that don't believe are both correct. The believers will receive and the non-believers won't. Both will get what they say and believe.

Now let's fast forward. Through the centuries, many mighty movements of God's Holy Spirit have occurred. A man by the name of Martin Luther started to preach salvation by faith alone and the whole country that became Germany was converted. Various revivals occurred in Europe through the ages. In America preachers by the name of Wesley, Whitefield, and others were used by the Holy Spirit to bring what is called the Great Awakening or Great Revival in what was largely rural frontier America in the eighteenth and nineteenth centuries. Like the other times, not all people participated. But large enough numbers of people did which brought great change and blessing to our nation.

One such great preacher was a man by the name of Charles Grandison Finney (1792-1875). This man of God saw revival break out wherever he often went to call people to repentance. Miracles took place. In his book, *Power From God* (Copyright 1996, Whitaker House), Finney has a chapter titled, "The Spirit Falls on Sodom." At the request of a female missionary society, Mr. Finney came to a town in upstate New York shortly after he was licensed to preach.

Mr. Finney visited around the town and found the wickedness of the community deserving of its name: Sodom. With no churches or religious meetings held in the village, Finney after much prayer with "groaning," commenced to preach the Word of God. He states that "an instantaneous shock seemed to fall upon the congregation." Then, "The power from on high came down upon them in such a torrent that they fell from their seats in every direction. In less that a minute, nearly all the people in the congregation were either down on their knees or on their faces or in some position prostrate before God. Everyone was crying or groaning for mercy upon his own soul." Finney ends the chapter with this: "Those who have lived in that region can testify to the permanent results of that blessed revival. I can only give in words a feeble description of that wonderful manifestation of power from on high that attended the preaching of the Word." Sounds a lot like the book of Acts, doesn't it?

In the days of this twenty-first century, the Holy Ghost continues to move mightily in great revivals. Reinhard Bonnke has seen untold thousands experience what Finney talked about. Most of Bonnke's revivals have occurred in Africa, where up to one million souls have given their lives to Christ in a single meeting! Again, not everyone participated with the Holy Spirit. Some in America might even doubt the numbers or the miracles that occurred, such as healings, gifts of the Holy Ghost, and salvation. "Those things don't happen anymore," they say.

I have often wondered in the past why it always seemed that God would move in a big way at a time or place where I wasn't. Example: a person comes to church and speaks of a great revival that took place in Africa, or some far away place where I was not present. Or another speaks of a great Spiritual movement taking place in China. Ever notice how the big numbers always take place somewhere else?

"I sure would like it Lord if I could witness your Spirit moving in great power over multitudes," was a frequent prayer of mine years ago, and still is. It was only *after* being filled with His Spirit did God answer my prayer.

I was part of a missionary group of thirty men who traveled from the USA to Colombia for 2 weeks. We met with approximately 30-40 people that were nationals of this South American country. We visited Bogota and Cali in what became one of the largest Bible distributions in the world. One would think that these two cities would not be the best places in the world for a great move of the Holy Spirit. Yet, the Holy Spirit enabled this relatively small group of men to give out 716,150 Scriptures. These were given out one at a time! The soul winning that accompanied these distributions resulted in 19,167 decisions for Christ! These decisions weren't with large evangelistic meetings, but with individuals and small groups (students, soldiers). My prayer was answered!

Having prayed with hundreds practically every day of that two weeks, I was able to witness one of the great movements of the Holy Ghost in our day. Brother and sister-it doesn't necessarily happen just to others. It can happen to you and me-if we allow the Holy Spirit to fill us. This group of men prayed daily, beginning at 5:00 a.m. We called upon the Holy Spirit to fill us and went out in His power and authority to where He placed us. Big things just happened!

Remember, if one person is led to Christ (the Anointed), that is a miracle of the Holy Ghost. When done in large numbers, that is a great movement of the Holy Ghost. But to each individual who receives, it is miraculous. At what point it becomes a great movement is difficult to say.

One of the days I was in Cali, four of us went to a large school. This school was composed of several open buildings, each housing different classes of children. The entire campus was fenced in and guarded, as is their custom in

Colombia. We went from classroom to classroom, giving a Gospel presentation from the back of the testaments we were giving to the students. Scores of students in each class responded to the Holy Spirit's prompting and prayed to receive Christ. Interestingly, the school principal followed us around the campus but said very little, though she heard the presentation several times. At the end of the school visit, I presented her a copy of God's Word. I remarked that she had heard the presentation so many times, that she could probably give it herself. "Yes, I believe I could," she replied in her native Spanish. I then asked what was holding her back from making a commitment to Jesus. "Nothing," she answered. At this point in full view of students and teachers, this principal gave her life to God.

Then the Holy Spirit came down upon her and she started jumping up and down with excitement, shouting "Hallelujah!" Jesus' promise of receiving power to witness was fulfilled within seconds as she immediately went up to two teachers and told them, "You need to give your life to Jesus, also!" She opened up the back of her testament and went through the plan of salvation and soon both teachers were bowing their heads in prayer becoming Christians! The principal wasn't a Christian more than 5 minutes and had already won two people to the Lord! The last thing I saw as I left the school was the principal talking with her secretary about the need for salvation. A miracle took place for each individual; several individuals were involved. Multiply this several times and one could say it was a great move of God.

Chapter 16

THE HOLY GHOST IN JAIL

⌒⧽⌒

One of my favorite movings of the Holy Spirit takes place in the book of Acts, chapter 16. Here Paul and Silas are thrown in prison at Philippi. Not only were they mishandled, but they were placed in the inner part of the prison, with their feet fastened in stocks. Things were not looking very favorable for these two Christians. Many Christians in their place would weep and give up: not Paul and Silas!

But at midnight Paul and Silas were praying and singing hymns to God, and the prisoners were listening to them. Suddenly there was a great earthquake, so that the foundations of the prison were shaken; and immediately all the doors were opened and everyone's chains were loosed.
Acts 16:25, 26 NKJV

These men were filled with the Holy Ghost, singing hymns and making melody in their hearts to the Lord (Ephesians 5:19). The Spirit moved and they were freed and at least one family was saved. The Holy Ghost often moves in jails and prisons.

I am privileged to visit jails and witness to the incarcer-ated. We typically go into cell blocks of thirty to fifty pris-oners, with two or three soul winners serving. We hand out New Testaments, with one or two people giving their testi-mony, followed by a Gospel presentation, ending with an invitation to receive Christ. There are times when few pris-oners have confessed Christ in jail, and times when hundreds have come to him in a single morning. Each prisoner who receives Christ is a miracle, and at times I have witnessed hundreds of miracles. On the days of huge response, there have always been some Christians witnessing to the pris-oners who lead nobody to salvation, while other witnesses see multitudes come into the Kingdom. Why is that? One can have several groups of Christians that are in jail to witness; some get results and some don't. What is the difference? Early on it came to me that those who believed in the baptism of the Holy Ghost saw large numbers of converts come to Jesus while those who didn't believe in Spirit baptism saw few or none. Holy Ghost power (Acts 1:8) made the difference! If you, reader, have never led people to Christ, could it be there is no power present? Let me ask you a question. Would this be up to you or God?

I often say that an empty room (or church building) doesn't have the Holy Ghost till the first believer comes in. Now, obviously God is ever present in every place. But that isn't what I'm talking about. Let's try to make theology practical. When you, a Christian, enter a room, the Holy Ghost enters also, only this time in a human body. No matter what ungodly place exists, no matter how evil a place is, the moment you appear the Holy Ghost appears on the scene. This is one of the greatest confidence builders God has given us:

The Holy Spirit is present in your every circumstance.

I don't care where you are or what trouble you are in, the Holy Spirit is present in your every circumstance. If you have confessed your sins and asked for the Holy Spirit filling, the Holy Ghost is now coming out of your belly for service (John 7:38). Something is going to happen! The living water is pouring forth from your belly to accomplish God's will. Now, how confident should you be? It doesn't matter if all hell is against you; you and the Holy Ghost will accomplish great things. Like Paul and Silas, God is going to move heaven and earth for your benefit.

I am not talking about "feeling" the presence of the Holy Spirit. I'm talking about a confident knowledge of the Holy Spirit's presence even if it doesn't "feel" like He is there. At times like these, God will always honor His Word even if we don't "feel" like He is on the scene. Now I love the feeling of God's presence wherever it is. I love to be in the presence of God! But there can be times when we are under the devil's attack and we just don't feel God's presence. Jesus surely knew the feeling when He cried out:

> *"MY God, my God, why hast Thou forsaken me?"*
> *Mark 15:34*

God is on the scene nevertheless. When the demons of hell are doing their best to bring you down, you must believe that God is present and that He will come to your assistance. This is Bible faith.

> *But without faith it is impossible to please Him: for he that cometh to God must believe that He is, and that He is a rewarder of them that diligently seek Him.*
> *Hebrews 11:6*

It is pleasing to God when we by faith come to Him even when it just doesn't look like He is around. That is what faith is. Faith is the evidence that God is present, even when you can't see or feel Him.

> *Now faith is the substance of things hoped for,*
> *the evidence of things not seen. For by it the elders*
> *obtained a good report.*
>
> *Hebrews 11:1,2*

God will always honor your faith. You may only have the faith of a mustard seed, but God will honor it, because He always honors His Word. Christian brother or sister, when you are down and God doesn't seem to be around, by faith believe that He is and start acting like He's there with you. You may have to speak the Word of God into a situation to come out victoriously. At the point where it looks like the devil and his hoards have you where they want you, you begin speaking God's presence into the calamity and watch the power of God bring you great deliverance. What looks like a victory for Satan, turns into his defeat and your victory.

A great example of this is from one of the darkest days of my life which turned out to be one of the greatest days. I went from absorbing all that Satan could muster against me, to watching God bring wonderful deliverance and salvation. It began with me going through airport security in a large city where it was discovered my handgun was in my carry-on baggage. I had forgotten to put the gun away after target practice one weekend, leaving it in my overnight bag. In a hurry to get to the airport, I grabbed my overnight bag, stuffed it with the clothes I was bringing, and never thought of checking the side pocket. Arriving at the airport, one moment I was putting my bag into the x-ray device and the next I was under arrest and charged with a felony! The following 24 hours I went to three different jails, received rough treatment, and pondered a future of years in jail. I felt like Job: all was going well until calamity suddenly struck. The devil thought he had me out of commission, and I had "feelings" that he was right on this account. I was wrong to agree with the devil. When all of hell breaks loose, we have a tendency to feel weak and without hope. I was not feeling very "spiritual."

After 20 hours of humiliation, stark conditions, and great loneliness, I felt compelled to "do something." God's Spirit felt a long ways away, even though in reality He was in me and with me. The devil was telling me, "Your ministry is over. You are going to lose your profession. You will never be able to vote again. Your children will grow up several years without you. Kids will pick on them at school for having a "jail-bird" for a father. How will your wife manage without you?" The prosecuting attorneys agreed with what the devil was saying. According to them, prison was my future. They didn't listen to my explanation; they wanted to make an example of me. What was I going to do?

The only thing I could do was to quote Scripture. I couldn't change my circumstances or situation, but I could at least bring God's Holy Word into the mess I found myself in. Someday you may find yourself in a predicament where no Bible is present. The only Word of God you will have is that which you have memorized. And the faith you will have will only come from the Word you hear or say.

So then faith cometh by hearing, and hearing by the Word of God.

Romans 10:17

At these times one must speak out the Word of God to the devil and any barrier that is keeping us bound. Jesus said to speak to the obstacle, whether it be a tree or a mountain.

"And the Lord said, 'If you had faith as mustard seed, you can say to this mulberry tree, "Be pulled up by the roots and be planted in the sea,' and it would obey you."

Luke 17:6 NKJV

So Jesus answered and said to them, "Assuredly, I say to you, if you have faith and do not doubt, you will not only do what was done to the fig tree, but also if you say to this mountain, 'Be removed and be cast into the sea,' it will be done. And whatever things you ask in prayer, believing, you will receive."

Matthew 21:21, 22 NKJV

I had been placed in a large holding area with over 40 prisoners, waiting for my first court appearance. Under great duress, having no sleep for two days, I got off the dirty floor(there were no seats), and began to pace back and forth quoting Scripture out loud in front of the rest of the prisoners.

In righteousness shalt thou be established: thou shalt be far from oppression; for thou shalt not fear: and from terror; for it shall not come near thee.

No weapon that is formed against thee shall prosper; and every tongue that shall rise against thee in judgment thou shalt condemn. This is the heritage of the servants of the Lord, and their righteousness is of Me, saith the Lord.

Isaiah 54:14,17

I would walk back and forth repeating the Word of God. I would then quote the ninety-first Psalm. I speak this Psalm aloud frequently, personalizing it.

114

I dwell in the secret place of the Most High, and I abide under the shadow of the Almighty. I say of the Lord, "You are my refuge and my fortress. My God, in you I trust. Surely you will deliver me from the snare of the fowler and from the noisome pestilence. You cover me with your feathers and under your wings I trust. Your truth is my shield and buckler." I am not afraid of the terror that comes by night nor the arrow that flies by day. I am not afraid of the pestilence that walks in darkness, nor the destruction that wastes at noonday. A thousand shall fall at my side, and ten thousand by my right hand, but it shall not come near me. Only with my eyes will I behold and see the reward of the wicked. Because I have made the Lord, which is my refuge, even the Most High my habitation, no evil shall befall me, neither any plague come near my dwelling. For He gives his angels charge over me, to keep me in all my ways. They bear me up, lest I dash my foot against a stone. "Because I have set my love upon you, you will deliver me; you will set me on high, because I have known your Name. When I call on you, you answer me, you are with me in trouble, you deliver me and you honor me. With long life do you satisfy me and show me your salvation."

I didn't care what the forty rough characters thought about me. The last vestiges of privacy and decency had been stripped away. I needed a mighty outpouring of the Holy Ghost and called out the Word of God. For years I had preached and taught about God honoring His Word, and that it never returns to Him void, but accomplishes that which He pleases and prospers in the place He sends it (Isaiah 55:11). The Holy Spirit was about to show me His power in a way I couldn't have imagined.

For several minutes I was pacing back and forth speaking the Word of God when I opened my eyes and saw a man standing in front of me with tears in his eyes. "Will you pray for me, mister?" he asked. "Certainly," I replied, as I laid hands on him. We prayed for God's forgiveness and salvation for this young criminal. When we had finished, I looked up and saw another man standing behind the first, who asked for the same. I laid hands on him and prayed in a like manner, not knowing that a line was beginning to form! Before I was finished, I had prayed with all but one prisoner. Forty men prayed for forgiveness and salvation in that dark place. Now the presence of the Holy Ghost was felt! Nobody felt Him an hour before, but now 40 did! Yet He was in that place the moment I walked in. His presence in not determined by our feelings. It is determined by our faith and His Word.

"This story is out of the book of Acts!" a friend has said. And so it is. The book of Acts can be called the book of the Acts of the Holy Spirit. I believe what the devil meant for evil, God meant for good. I was put there to witness to forty men who may not have otherwise received the Gospel. Within time I was released, found to be not guilty of purposefully carrying a firearm through security, with the judge deciding all records of the incident be "expunged." Earthly records show nothing happened that day. Heaven records great rejoicing took place that day, as the Holy Spirit had another movement.

So shall my word be that goeth forth out of my mouth: it shall not return unto me void, but it shall accomplish that which I please, and it shall prosper in the thing whereto I sent it.

Isaiah 55:11

116

Chapter 17

TONGUES

⟨∼⟩

In this chapter I will deal with the topic on tongues. Undoubtedly, some will pick up this book and turn to this chapter first. They will read the first few sentences and then judge the book by what little they read. Then they will decide to read the book based on my siding with their preconceived ideas on tongues. My purposes in writing this book were to honor the Holy Spirit and to accurately teach about the Holy Spirit's relationship to the believer. I will attempt to do both as I teach on this topic, which has often led to arguments and problems within the Church of Jesus Christ.

Let me start out with saying many born again Christians do not speak in tongues. Speaking in tongues never has been a qualification for salvation. If you are a Christian, you will go to heaven if you don't speak in tongues. In heaven you will speak in tongues, as I don't believe any earthly language will be used. In first Corinthians 13:1, there is reference to angels having different tongues or languages than people. So Christian, you will eventually speak in a tongue or language that is unknown to you. We can then say that all Christians will eventually become Pentecostal! You just don't have to die to get to that point! Obviously, God meant for us to speak in tongues here on earth, or He wouldn't have given us tongues. Tongues are for today. They are for our good and will be with us believers at least until *"that which is perfect has come." 1 Cor 13:10 NKJV*

Maybe we can simplify the teaching on tongues and find some common ground. If we pray that the Spirit of Truth will reveal what He wants to us, we will be on the right track. Let us be like the Bereans, and search the Scriptures to see what the Word of God says about this important topic.

In my understanding, the Bible teaches that there are three types or divisions of tongues. A Christian may speak with all three, or with only one or two, or with none. When I first came to Christ, I didn't speak with any. I didn't know anything about it. When I first heard about tongues, I thought it was for weirdoes! I would even argue with Pentecostal people that tongues ceased after the Bible was written, that it was no longer a part of the Church, etc. It is hard to argue with somebody that speaks in tongues that there isn't such a thing! When I gained greater understanding it became very clear. Part of the understanding is dividing tongues into the three categories.

TONGUES-THE INITIAL EVIDENCE

I don't know of any Bible students who would dispute that tongues was not the initial evidence of the filling with the Holy Ghost at Pentecost. As we have previously learned, those in the upper room were already Christians and had received the Holy Spirit (John 20:22). Jesus had told them before His ascension, that they would be baptized with the Holy Spirit in a few days (Acts 1:5). He told them that they would receive power after the Holy Spirit came *upon* them, not in them. Then in Acts 2 His prophecy came to be.

And when the day of Pentecost was fully come, they were all with one accord in one place. And suddenly there came a sound from heaven as of a rushing mighty wind, and it filled all the house where they were sitting. And there appeared unto them cloven tongues like as of fire, and it sat upon each of them. And they were all filled with the Holy Ghost, and began to speak with other tongues, as the Spirit gave them utterance.

Acts 2:1-4

It is obvious that something was evident when the Holy Spirit sat on them: they spoke in tongues. It was the Spirit that gave them the utterance, or ability to speak. The Bible doesn't say whether the people doing the speaking understood what they were saying, but people of other languages heard the *wonderful works of God* coming from the mouths of those who didn't know the languages. All were amazed, yet some mocked at this movement of the Holy Spirit. Dear reader, don't be among the mockers.

There were many languages represented. God made sure He got their attention! A true Pentecostal tongue was in a language others could understand. However, the Bible is silent about whether there were tongues being spoken that weren't understood. It only says that those unbelievers heard their own language. The main point I want to make is that speaking in tongues was the evidence of their filling of the Holy Spirit. Had they not spoken in tongues, who would have known they were filled? For those readers who don't think tongues are important, try taking tongues out of Acts 2 and make sense of Pentecost. Peter told his audience,

"Therefore being exalted to the right hand of God, and having received from the Father the promise of the Holy Spirit, He poured out this which you now see and hear."

Acts 2:33 NKJV

They could see and hear the evidence of the filling. But this evidence was not to be restricted to only the day of Pentecost. It was not to be restricted to the Jews only. When Peter traveled to Caesarea, he preached to the family and friends of Cornelius, a believing Roman.

> *While Peter was still speaking these words, the Holy Spirit fell upon all those who heard the word. And those of the circumcision who believed were astonished, as many as came with Peter, because the gift of the Holy Spirit had been poured out on the Gentiles also. For they heard them speak with tongues and magnify God. Then Peter answered, "Can anyone forbid water, that these should not be baptized who have received the Holy Spirit just as we have?"*
>
> *Acts 10:44-47 NKJV*

How did the Jews know that the Gentiles had the Holy Spirit upon them? Because *they heard them speak with tongues and magnify God.* Peter said that these Gentiles had *"received the Holy Spirit just as we have."*

In a previous chapter we talked about Paul visiting Ephesus in Acts 19. There Paul found disciples who had not received the filling of the Holy Ghost. The Pentecost experience had not yet occurred in Ephesus. Some well meaning Christians say that the Holy Spirit came at Pentecost and has stayed with the Christian Church ever since. If this is true, then the Holy Spirit missed Ephesus and went everywhere else.

> *He said to them, "Did you receive the Holy Spirit when you believed?" So they said to him, "We have not so much as heard whether there is a Holy Spirit."*

120

And when Paul had laid hands on them, the Holy
Spirit came upon them, and they spoke with tongues
and prophesied.
Acts 19:2, 6 NKJV

What was the evidence of the Holy Ghost filling? They
spoke in tongues and prophesied. There are places in the
Bible where they were filled with the Holy Ghost and spoke
the Word of God boldly. Whether they spoke in tongues
or not isn't mentioned, however the *initial* evidence of the
filling is accompanied with tongues, whether people understood the language or not. The filling of the Holy Spirit was
evidenced at Ephesus like it was at Jerusalem.

The whole book of Acts should be read with this understanding. Then we see the whole picture of the evidence of
the baptism of the Holy Spirit. Philip came to Samaria and
preached salvation to the Samaritans. They believed and then
were baptized. When Peter and John heard about it,

Who, when they had come down, prayed for them
that they might receive the Holy Spirit. For as yet He
had fallen upon none of them. They had only been
baptized in the name of the Lord Jesus. Then they laid
hands on them, and they received the Holy Spirit.
Acts 8:15-17 NKJV

Although speaking in tongues isn't specifically
mentioned, if the experience was the same as the one previously mentioned, they would have. How else would anyone
know they were filled? And if nothing happened with the
initial filling, why did Simon the Sorcerer see the evidence
and want to buy the Holy Spirit's power (Acts 8:18,19)?

Let me make a statement: *It is the Biblical norm for people*
to speak with tongues with their initial filling or baptism of
the Holy Spirit. It did not end at Pentecost; it only began

there. From Jerusalem speaking in tongues was evidenced in Caesarea, Samaria, Ephesus, Corinth, to eventually the United States and your town or city. Denying this fact of Christianity does not make the fact go away.

Let God be true, but every man a liar.

Romans 3:4b

Does God allow other evidences of this filling when tongues are not present? He has in many instances. The power to win souls to Christ is an evidence. It's not an immediate evidence, but does show a supernatural empowering to witness as Jesus said. But why not speak in tongues? The answer is that some never heard about speaking in tongues, and some like myself were taught by well meaning pastors and teachers NOT to speak in tongues. "Speaking in tongues is of the devil!" Well, I certainly didn't want that then! But as years went by, I came to realize that in the Bible the devil didn't speak with tongues, only the Spirit-filled believers did! My initial filling was not evidenced with tongues. I wouldn't allow it. Reader, you can be filled with the Holy Spirit without speaking in tongues also, but why would you want to?

TONGUES-THE PRAYER LANGUAGE

The second category pertaining to tongues is the prayer language. People unfamiliar with tongues often confuse the three categories of tongues: the initial evidence of the filling, the praying with the filling, and the gift of tongues which comes with the filling. When looking at them separately, it isn't nearly as confusing, even for the Christian who isn't filled.

Anything I can do to improve my prayer with my God is important. I used to think that praying in English was enough. "Why should I pray or sing in tongues?" I would ask myself.

It didn't make sense to me. If I don't understand what I am praying, what is the use? The answer is that there are some things I can't know, or never will know, until I pray regardless of my lack of knowledge. There are things God has for me that I can't hear, see, or even begin to understand.

Paul talks of this in 1 Corinthians, chapter 2.

> *But as it is written, Eye hath not seen, nor ear heard, neither have entered into the heart of man, the things which God hath prepared for them that love Him. But God hath revealed them unto us by his Spirit: for the Spirit searcheth all things, yea, the deep things of God. For what man knoweth the things of a man, save the spirit of man which is in him: even so the things of God knoweth no man, but the Spirit of God. Now we have received, not the spirit of the world, but the Spirit of God; that we might know the things that are freely given to us of God. Which things also we speak, not in the words which man's wisdom teacheth, but which the Holy Ghost teacheth; comparing spiritual things with spiritual. But the natural man receiveth not the things of the Spirit of God: for they are foolishness unto him: neither can he know them, because they are spiritually discerned. But he that is spiritual judgeth all things, yet he himself is judged of no man.*
>
> *1 Cor 2:9-15*

Some things the Holy Spirit can only teach without man's imput. The natural man is unsaved, or may be a man proclaiming to be a Christian, but for all appearances is living *naturally,* and not *spiritually.* Anything spiritual cannot be received by such a person, as it is foolishness to him. It is impossible for this person to hear the things of the Spirit, as he has the spirit of the world in control.

One modern translation, the New Living Translation puts it this way:

> *When we tell you this, we do not use words of human wisdom. We speak words given to us by the Spirit, using the Spirit's words to explain spiritual truths.*
>
> *Or*
>
> *.......explaining spiritual truths in spiritual language.*
>
> *1 Cor 2:13 NLT*

Another way of saying this, is that when we pray in tongues, we let out Spiritual truth that is inside us, because the Holy Spirit is inside us. Our natural brain is not capable of discerning the deep things of God. The act of praying in tongues will often reveal things that we need to know: things that won't be known any other way.

In another place Paul says:

> *For if I pray in an unknown tongue, my spirit prayeth, but my understanding is unfruitful. What is it then: I will pray with the spirit, and I will pray with the understanding also: I will sing with the spirit, and I will sing the understanding also.*
>
> *1 Cor 14:14,15*

Here our Lord is teaching us that we should pray with understanding, but also with an unknown tongue, or pray in the Spirit. When praying in the Spirit, you won't know what you are praying for, as your understanding is unfruitful. But when you are finished praying, you will have greater insight on spiritual things. Often something that was hidden is brought to light. The spiritual core of a problem is often revealed. You will learn things that you had no way of knowing without praying in the Spirit. Let's make it really simple: if one knew what he was praying when in the Spirit, it wouldn't be an *unknown* tongue.

I tell students that if it sounds uncomfortable when praying in the Spirit, they are probably doing it correctly! After all, it seems foolish to the natural person. This is a key to praying in the Spirit: at first it will seem foolish or weird. That's because it is! Get over it. You've done other weird things in your life. This isn't the first nor will it be the last.

Another benefit from praying in tongues is building up your faith. Now faith comes from hearing the Word of God, which is the Bible. But praying in the Spirit releases God's Word also, even if we can't comprehend it. The Word is going forth nevertheless.

But ye, beloved, building up yourselves on your most holy faith, praying in the Holy Ghost, keep yourselves in the love of God, looking for the mercy of our Lord Jesus Christ unto eternal life.

Jude 20

After praying in the Holy Spirit, you will be built up in your faith. Your confidence in whatever you are facing will rise. You will be edified:

He who speaks in a tongue edifies himself, but he who prophesies edifies the church.

1 Cor 14:4 NKJV

I can hear the doubter now say, "I feel better when I pray now. I don't need to do it in a prayer language." You, dear friend, are correct. You don't need to. But why would you want to limit the Holy Spirit in your life, when He wants to speak to you and build you up?

Let's try something. You get into your prayer closet where nobody can hear you. In private, tell the Holy Spirit that you want to follow the Bible and pray in tongues. He will honor the request. Then you begin to speak weird noises from your mouth, repeating unintelligible syllables. God won't do it or make you do it; you will have to do the "foolish" thing and try to speak. He won't take over your speaking apparatus, you do the speaking. I used to sit in silence, waiting for God to have me speak in tongues. "If you want me to speak in tongues, you will have to do it Lord." Nothing ever happened. It was up to me, not God. I had to speak, with the Spirit giving me utterance. He gave me the sounds to say and I had to say them! It will be the same for you.

After feeling peculiar, try it again another time soon. The more you do it the more familiar you will be doing it. The first time you prayed in English you weren't too hot either! Soon you will be experiencing *praying in the Holy Ghost* as a regular part of your prayer life. It will not take away praying in English from you. You may find that praying in English is even better now that you pray in tongues also. Many times when I am praying in English and I forget something I should be praying for, I will pray in the Spirit till my mind remembers and I will finish the prayer in English. A whole new avenue awaits you. Go for it! Learning to pray in tongues is similar to learning to pray in your own language. It takes practice.

TONGUES-THE GIFT

The gift of tongues is given for the benefit of the whole church, not the individual. Along with this gift comes the necessary gift of interpretation of tongues. A Christian may have one or the other, or both gifts, or none of these two "charismatic" gifts. We will learn more of the different gifts in a later chapter.

The gift of tongues we find in the Bible in 1 Corinthians, chapters 12, 13, and 14. Paul starts out chapter 12 with:

> *Now concerning spiritual gifts, brethren, I do not want you to be ignorant:*
> *1 Cor 12:1 NKJV*

and ends chapter 14 with:

> *...do not forbid to speak with tongues. Let all things be done decently and in order.*
> *1 Cor 14:39,40 NKJV*

It is therefore logical that God wants us to know about spiritual gifts, including tongues, and that Christians should not forbid the practice of tongues. But the speaking in tongues should be done decently and in order. There is a proper place for speaking in tongues. Let the Bible be the guide.

Let's clear up a few misconceptions about tongues. You and I have heard all kinds of arguments for and against tongues. One pastor told me that he believed that the two books of Corinthians were just for the Corinthian church: that tongues did not pertain to the rest of Christianity, only Corinth. I countered that I knew he was smarter than that. If that were true, then Romans would be only for the city of Rome, Ephesians only for Ephesus, and first and second Timothy were only for one person: Timothy! And if Paul meant it only for the Corinthians, why did he in the beginning of the first chapter of 1 Corinthians (verse 2) say that the letter was for the church of God at Corinth and for

> *...all who in every place call on the name of Jesus Christ...?.*
> *1 Cor 1:2 NKJV*

Others have said that tongues ceased when the last apostle died. Where this argument came from nobody knows, but somebody read it somewhere! They just didn't read it in the Bible. When Paul wrote the letters to the Corinthians there were *still* apostles being appointed (1 Cor 12:28). When Paul wrote the book to the Ephesian church there were *still* apostles being appointed (Eph 4:11). Just as the gifts of the Holy Ghost were never done away with, neither was the gift of the apostle. If God did away with apostles, then the prophets, evangelists, pastors, and teachers somehow left also, because they are listed in the same passages. That is like saying that Billy Graham is not an evangelist, because God did away with evangelists in the first century! This argument doesn't hold water.

"Well, tongues ceased because it says *tongues will cease* (1 Cor 13:8)." Tell that to someone who speaks in tongues! In that same verse it states that knowledge will vanish also. With this argument, we would have to say that there are no tongues in the world, and nobody knows anything! This type of reasoning doesn't deserve much time either. Knowledge is increasing in this world. When the *PERFECT* has come (verse 10), we won't need tongues nor the interpretation of such. We won't need a lot of things we need today. But He hasn't come yet.

Chapter 18

THE GIFTS OF
THE HOLY SPIRIT-PART 1

I n the chapter, "The Fruit Of The Spirit," it was mentioned that the fruit demonstrates who the person is and the gifts tell what the person does. Jesus said:

> *Ye shall know them by their fruits.*
>
> *Matthew 7:16*

The fruit of the Spirit is love, joy, peace, longsuffering, gentleness, goodness, faith, meekness, and temperance (Galatians 5:22, 23). The fruit will demonstrate that a person is a Christian. The Holy Spirit is living in that person. That is what the person is. Example: he is a loving person; she is a joyful person; he is a peaceful person, etc. The gifts of the Spirit show how the Christian *performs*. The gifts tell what the person does. They are gifts of service to others. The fruit of the Spirit can often be seen by the gifts of the Spirit.

I am not talking about natural talents. While talents are gifts from God also, they are not limited to born again, Spirit-filled believers. Non-believers can have God-given talents. But the true gifts of the Holy Spirit come when the Holy

Spirit comes into and especially upon people. Then these Spirit-filled people can accomplish great things in service to God: things they couldn't do before the filling. Some of these things or works can be greater than what Jesus did:

> *Verily, verily, I say unto you, He that believeth me the works that I do shall he do also, and greater works than these shall he do, because I go unto my Father.*
>
> *John 14:12*

This is a hard saying: that believers will actually do greater works than Jesus. Since Jesus said it, we know that it is true. How can this be? The answer is that believers are doing the work of Jesus when they do the actual works in the power of Jesus' Holy Spirit. The believer is not doing things better than the One believed in; the One believed in is doing the work through the believer. Sometimes the works that Jesus does through a Spirit-filled believer's body is greater than what He did from His own earth-suit. That is rightly understanding the John 14:12 verse.

Jesus had all the gifts of the Holy Spirit. He operated in the *fullness* of the Spirit, never failed in his duties, could and did accomplish all that He set out to do.

> *For it pleased the Father that in him should all fulness dwell;*
>
> *Colossians 1:19*

> *For in him dwelleth all the fulness of the Godhead bodily.*
>
> *Colossians 2:9*

Jesus had all knowledge of His power and authority. He operated in full faith. He had the full faith of God without measure. While we have the faith of God, our faith is measured, or limited. John the Baptist, filled with the Holy Ghost while in his mother's womb (Luke 1:15), realized his shortcomings when compared to Jesus, and said of Jesus:

> *"For he is sent by God. He speaks God's word, for*
> *God's Spirit is upon him without measure or limit."*
> *John 3:34 NLT*

Regarding the faith of the believer, the Bible says:

> *....God hath dealt to every man the measure of*
> *faith.*
> *Romans 12:3b*

> *But unto every one of us is given grace according*
> *to the measure of the gift of Christ.*
> *Ephesians 4:7*

Because of our measured/limited faith, we don't have all the gifts of the Holy Spirit in each of us, like Jesus did. Therefore to form a complete body, all believers need to join together to accomplish what Jesus could and does today. We are His body. His body today is not weaker than His body was two thousand years ago. It is just fragmented! When complete, we accomplish even greater things than He could when he walked in his earth-suit. That is why a study of the gifts of the Holy Spirit is so important. All the gifts, when put together, are the full expression of the Holy Ghost in this day. That is how the Holy Ghost operates. Why certain churches would not want to encourage the expression of these gifts must even make Jesus wonder! Some churches will throw people out of the congregation for operating in the gifts. Surely the Holy Spirit is grieved, if not blasphemed. The Holy Spirit is not welcomed in some churches.

The gifts of the Holy Spirit are listed for the most part in three places in the Bible: Ephesians 4:11, Romans 12, and 1 Corinthians 12 and 14. Gifts listed in one scripture are not greater than gifts listed somewhere else. Let's take a brief overview of the generally accepted gifts listed in Ephesians.

Ephesians 4:8-13

Wherefore he saith, When he ascended up on high, he led captivity captive, and gave gifts unto men. (Now that he ascended, what is it but that he also descended first into the lower parts of the earth? He that descended is the same also that ascended up far above all heavens, that he might fill all things.) And he gave some, apostles; and some, prophets; and some, evangelists; and some, pastors and teachers; for the perfecting of the saints, for the work of the ministry, for the edifying of the body of Christ; Till we all come in the unity of the faith, and of the knowledge of the Son of God, unto a perfect man, unto the measure of the stature of the fulness of Christ:

Jesus said that when He went up to heaven, He would send the Comforter, who was the Holy Spirit, who came on the day of Pentecost. In the above scripture, it states that He also gave gifts for the perfecting or equipping the saints (or believers) for ministry and edifying or building up the body of Christ. The five gifts listed are then ministry gifts for the church body. They are often referred to as the five-fold ministry gifts. They will be necessary till we are all of unity of the faith and to the measure of the fullness of Christ, till we as saints are perfected. We need these gifts now more than ever. These gifts are also commonly occupational in the church. They can be full-time positions.

Pastors, teachers, and evangelists are probably the most accepted in modern Christianity, even by those churches not emphasizing the Holy Spirit. But call someone an apostle or a prophet, and many Christians will give you a puzzled look or will maintain a strange silence. Some will even argue that there are no more apostles or prophets. They just can't say when the two gifts disappeared. They were in existence at the time Ephesians was written. The above scripture says they will be with us *till we all come in the unity of the faith.* Obviously, we aren't there yet. If we had already reached perfection, then God would have done away with the pastor, teacher, and evangelist also. All five gifts are with us today. Many Christians have only a pastor or a teacher in their church. They aren't operating with all the gifts. I can get by without my legs. But I operate better with them. I could get by without my sight, but not as well. Many churches are crippled and blind because they don't have all the gifts. They get by, but not very well. Any wonder why the modern church is so ineffective?

An apostle today is much like the apostle in New Testament times. They start new churches and ministries, and exercise leadership or authority over those areas. The Greek word *apostolos* means a person sent out. An apostle has the signs following we find in Mark 16. Paul said that signs, wonders, and mighty deeds accompanied the apostle (2 Corinthians 12:12). My pastor, Rev. Don Lyon, is also an apostle. Not only has he started multiple churches, he also began two Christian radio stations. Ministries for the poor and the addicted came from his ministry. Often the sick are healed in Apostle Lyon's services. Our church has a Christian school. Many other ministries are under the mantle of this apostle. He would be the first to say it was all of the Holy Spirit. But I would say that this man was gifted by the Holy Spirit to do the mighty deeds. He is an apostle.

The second gift of the 5-fold ministry is that of the prophet. The prophet is one who speaks forth the Word of God. A good example is Jonah. God told him to go to

Nineveh and preach repentance, which he did. We know that he didn't want to: that's why he was swallowed by the fish! But his message caused the inhabitants of the great city to repent of evil and violence, and God spared the city. This prophet spoke forth the Word of God. Sometimes, like in Jonah's case, great revival can come forth. Other times, like in Jeremiah's case, few will heed. Yet the person still speaks the truth, regardless of outcome. Like in the Old Testament, the prophet is not always liked, because he can step on people's toes. John the Baptist was a prophet, and the religious and governmental authorities didn't like him. There are strong prophets today who speak up and are ridiculed by the media and authorities. They won't change their message. It is from God. Their message can also be encouraging to the faithful. Like the other 4 gifts of Ephesians, the prophet is:

For the perfecting of the saints, for the work of the ministry, for the edifying of the body of Christ.
Ephesians 4:13

The evangelist is the one who brings the evangel-the good news to people. The evangelist is gifted by the Spirit to speak to others about salvation in Jesus Christ. He/she has the Spirit inspired words to say that will bring sinners to repentance. This can be before thousands/millions of people, like Billy Graham, or to one person at a time. You may have been won to the Lord by an evangelist's preaching, teaching, or writing. Maybe it was a one on one conversation with someone. That someone was either an evangelist or someone who *"did the work of an evangelist" (2 Timothy 4:5)*.

The pastor is the person gifted by the Spirit to "shepherd the flock" of believers. He may be called upon to teach, to evangelize, and to give prophetic messages. He may have to wear several hats! His primary focus is to minister to the spiritual welfare of his church or assembly. His job is to perfect the saints, edify the body of believers, and to work the ministry. How much better would the pastor be if he were helped by those ministering in their gifts. Let the pastor be the pastor, and allow the teacher to teach, the prophet to prophesy, the evangelist to evangelize, and the apostle to go out and start new missions. Many churches expect the pastor to do everything, allowing the members to sit back and complain about how nothing is happening at the church.

The teacher is the person gifted by God to teach the Church Biblical truth. The person is able to communicate and disseminate Biblical knowledge to students is a powerful way. This person loves to study the Word of God and delights in telling others what he/she has learned.

The 5-fold ministry will often use the gifts mentioned in Romans 12 and 1 Corinthians 12 as part of their ministry. Again, we will always need the 5-fold ministry:

Till we all come in the unity of the faith, and of the knowledge of the Son of God, unto a perfect man, unto the measure of the stature of the fulness of Christ.

Ephesians 4:13

Chapter 19

THE GIFTS OF
THE HOLY SPIRIT-PART 2

It has been said that the gifts mentioned in Ephesians 4 were sent down to earth from Jesus, that the gifts in 1 Corinthians were sent by the Spirit, and that the gifts in Romans 12 were sent by God (the Father). A distinction could be made and a long dissertation be written about something that may not be meant to be discussed. I don't want to be a part of conjecture. It may be interesting but not necessary as to the teaching of the gifts. Many of the gifts mentioned in one scripture are also mentioned in one or both of the others. For our purposes, all are gifts of the Holy Ghost.

For as we have many members in one body, and all members have not the same office: so we, being many, are one body in Christ, and every one members one of another. Having then gifts differing according to the grace that is given to us, whether prophecy, let us prophesy according to the proportion of faith; or ministry, let us wait on our ministering: or he that teacheth, on teaching; or he that exhorteth, on exhortation: he that giveth, let him do it with simplicity; he that ruleth, with diligence; he that sheweth mercy, with cheerfulness.

Romans 12: 4-8

Like in Ephesians, Paul teaches us the lesson of Christian unity: that we are all important members that need to work together. Each member of the body is to use his/her gifts in love (verse 9) and with the measure of faith (verse 3). We are many members of one body. I like the way the New Living Translation puts it:

So it is with Christ's body; We are all parts of his one body, and each of us has different work to do. And since we are all one body in Christ, we belong to each other, and each of us needs all the others.

Romans 12:5 NLT

Each of us needs all the others! Let's not try doing it alone. The gifts should never divide us but only unite us in service to our King. Let's take a quick look at these gifts. The gifts listed in Romans are often called the *service* gifts.

Prophecy: the speaking forth of the Word of God. The person gifted with prophecy will speak out what is right or wrong. It can often embarrass others. Sin may be exposed and others may get a confirmation of what God is already saying to them. The person's boldness may be *according to the proportion of faith* he or she has.

Ministry: the serving of others. The person with this gift loves to help or minister to others. He or she will always look to the needs of others. This person can't stand to see someone working and will always pitch in and help.

Teaching: imparting of knowledge or instruction. The person gifted in teaching loves to study the Bible and tell others. He/she will often want to share what he is currently reading and will volunteer to teach a class.

Exhorting: encouraging, urging, and advising. The person with this gift will come up to people and tell them, "Boy you did a good job! How do you do it?" The exhorter is the person who people gravitate around to feel good. They don't drag you down; they build you up.

Giving: handing out something a person owns to someone else. The verse implies a giver does it liberally. The giver can't keep anything, because she/he is always giving something away. A possession gives a giver more pleasure when she/he gives it away than when she/he keeps it.

Ruler: a leader or administrator. The ruler has the gift to find a need and then find the right person with the right gift to fill that need. He/she can take charge of a situation while others stand around and say, "Why doesn't somebody do something?"

Mercy: kindness above what would be expected. A person with the gift of mercy cheerfully reaches out to help others, regardless of need. This person will be quick to show tears and is the person who always feels sorry for the unfortunate.

These gifts are commonly called the service gifts, because they usually involve *doing*. All are needed and one is not more important than another. When asked what the most important Spiritual gift was, Oral Roberts reportedly said, "The one you need at the moment is the most important." Let's look at the gifts with the following example. Suppose I have a house with no garage for my automobile.

The prophet would tell me, "Hey, you really need a garage. You shouldn't leave your car out like that."

The minister or server would say, "Hey, do you need any help? Can I help you with building the garage?"

The teacher would say, "You know, I built one last year. Let me show you the plans I used."

The exhorter would say, "I know you can do it. You will build the best garage in the neighborhood!"

The giver would say, "Here are the tools for the project. Can I give you some of the needed materials?"

The ruler would tell me, "I know the best carpenter to help you. My brother is a roofer who is unemployed. The cement work should be done by Mr. Jones down the street, and let Bill Smith do the electrical part."

The person with mercy would say, "I feel so sorry for you. You probably get cold sitting in that unprotected car. Please use my garage till you get yours built."

Depending on my need, each person may be the most important at any given time. All may be needed. Can you see how the Body of Christ needs to work in unity? The use of the gifts will have us

Be kindly affectioned one to another with brotherly love; in honour preferring one another.

Romans 12:10

Chapter 20

THE GIFTS OF
THE HOLY SPIRIT-PART 3

*Now concerning spiritual gifts, brethren, I do not
want you to be ignorant:*
                                1 Corinthians 12:1 NKJV

I
t is amazing that there is such ignorance in the Christian
Church concerning the Spiritual gifts, when the Holy
Spirit expressly says, *"I don't want you to be ignorant."*
Those churches that do not preach and teach on the Spiritual
gifts are *ignorant.* Some do not know they are ignorant; they
lack the knowledge of the subject. They are unaware, inex-
perienced, and uneducated on the gifts. Others choose to be
ignorant. They don't *want* to be educated on the gifts. To
those people/churches/pastors I have a message of prophecy
from the Holy Spirit:

*Now concerning spiritual gifts, brethren, I do not
want you to be ignorant:*
                                1 Corinthians 12:1 NKJV

The Spiritual gifts mentioned in 1 Corinthians 12 and 14 are for today. Being ignorant of the gifts does not do away with the gifts; it just hinders the work of God in that group or assembly.

"Look how large our church is, and we don't teach the gifts," one may say. The work of God is hindered in your church.

"Look how many kids are in our Sunday School. We don't need the gifts!" The work of God is hindered in your church.

"We have a great senior's group, and our youth group is going well. We don't need to study the gifts!" The work of God is hindered in your church.

> *But the manifestation of the Spirit is given to each one for the profit of all:*
> *1 Corinthians 12:7 NKJV*

The gifts of the Spirit are to profit God's people. No matter where a person or church is in ministry, the gifts of the Spirit will profit above any ministry without the gifts. You will do and be better with the gifts of the Holy Ghost.

> *But the manifestation of the Spirit is given to each one for the profit of all: for to one is given the word of wisdom through the Spirit, to another gifts of healings by the same Spirit, to another the working of miracles, to another prophecy, to another discerning of spirits, to another different kinds of tongues, to another the interpretation of tongues. But one and the same Spirit works all these things, distributing to each one individually as He wills.*
> *1 Cor. 12:7-11 NKJV*

Paul goes on to say, as he did in Romans, that the gifts are of equal importance, and are joined together to form a body. The God of unity has put this together and doesn't want this body, His body, divided over the issue of gifts.

That there should be no schism in the body; but that the members should have the same care one for the other.

1 Corinthians 12:25

So let's look at these gifts that should be present in the Church and see how they can profit us. The nine gifts listed in 1 Corinthians can be divided into three groups of three gifts. They don't have to be divided like I will state, but it helps in the study of the gifts to see the similarities that exist. An excellent study of the gifts can be found in *The Holy Spirit And His Gifts*, by Kenneth E. Hagin (Copyright 1991, Rhema Bible Church, AKA Kenneth Hagin Ministries).

Revelational Gifts

The first group of Spiritual gifts we will discuss is the group of revelational gifts: the word of wisdom, the word of knowledge, and the discerning of spirits. We will call them the revelational gifts, because they reveal things when in operation which cannot be otherwise known.

Word of wisdom: the gift given to the believer to know the mind of the Holy Spirit in a given situation in order to use knowledge to affect the outcome. Someone operating in this gift knows what to do in a given situation. The Lord reveals a word of wisdom at the right time. "Why didn't I think of that?" is the question people ask when someone operates in this gift.

Word of knowledge: the gift the believer operates in that reveals certain facts and information by the Holy Spirit useful in service. The person operating in this gift can understand, analyze, and see things others can't. "How did you know that?" is frequently asked of those with this gift.

Discerning of spirits: the unique Spiritual gift that allows certain Christians to recognize or perceive the presence of spirit beings, good or evil. This gift allows the person to ascertain what may be motivating a behavior. "Did you see the demonic expression on his face?" a person with this gift might ask.

The three revelational gifts may work in synchrony. Often there is an overlap and the three gifts may not be easily separated. If someone can sense an evil motivation behind a person, may that also not be considered a word of knowledge? The Holy Spirit may also impart a word of wisdom in a situation that deals with the demonic, hence discerning of spirits.

Power Gifts

The gifts that we will call the power gifts are the gift of faith, the gifts of healings, and the gift of working miracles. These can be called power gifts because they often affect the physical world.

The gift of faith: that special ability to know with certainty the will and purpose of God in any situation. This is a supernatural ability to "see" what the Holy Spirit wants and the person sets his/her aspirations in that direction. Others can't see it, but the person with this gift "knows" what to do.

The gifts of healings: the gift whereby God uses certain individuals to bring about a cure for an ailment, whether it is physical, mental, or spiritual. Prayer is frequently used, as is the laying on of hands. The person may be given "cures" supernaturally that is offered to the ill person that affects a healing.

The gift of working miracles: the gift whereby a Christian intervenes supernaturally to change a course of nature. Frequently natural physical laws are superceded, or natural laws come into effect against tremendous odds to affect the change.

Again, these gifts can work closely together so that a clear distinction cannot always be made. Suppose a person is in a serious auto accident and loses a limb. She may by the gift of God have great faith that she will be rescued and will "hang on" till help comes against all human reason and experience. Someone gifted in healings may come by, lay hands on her, and the bleeding is stopped and her stump is healed, and she lives. The gifted worker of miracles may come by and with prayer a new limb grows back. That would be a miracle, not a healing. These gifts don't always work immediately. Sometimes they only work with proper timing. Sometimes a word of knowledge or wisdom is needed to know how to affect a healing. Can you see how the gifts work together?

Vocal Gifts

The vocal gifts are gifts used by the mouth and are the gifts of prophecy, tongues, and interpretation of tongues. Because they are spoken gifts, they are often attacked by the non-gifted. These three gifts are probably more often witnessed by others and viewed with suspicion.

Gift of prophecy: the speaking forth of the Word of God with divine unction. This may be to correct, to edify, or to warn of future events. The person with this gift is usually outspoken and is often considered judgmental. Sin can be cried out against, as well as faith being built up, as faith comes from the Word of God (Romans 10:17).

Gift of tongues: the gift whereby the individual speaks forth the Word of God in an unknown tongue or language. The person feels the urge to speak aloud in an assembly unintelligible words the he or she doesn't even understand.

Gift of interpretation: the gift whereby a hearer of tongues will have the unction of the Holy Spirit to speak out in the known language of the group what was the meaning or interpretation of the tongue. The gift of interpretation accompanies the gift of tongues. These three gifts work together for the same purpose: speaking out the Word of God. The one who prophesies

>...*speaks edification and exhortation and comfort to men.*
>
> *1 Cor. 14:3b NKJV*

All understand prophecy, even unbelievers. That is why it is superior to speaking in tongues (1Cor. 14:5, 24). A prophecy will never contradict the Bible or it is a false prophecy. People knowledgeable with the Scriptures should judge the content of the prophecy (1Cor. 14:29).

Speaking in tongues has the same effect as prophecy as it edifies, in this case, the individual (1 Cor. 14:4). The church is edified when the tongue is interpreted and the meaning is given to all. Therefore the gift of prophecy is essentially the same as the gifts of tongues and interpretation put together.

All the gifts of the Spirit noted in 1 Corinthians are important. The one you need in any given situation is the most important. But Paul said:

> *Pursue love, and desire spiritual gifts, but especially that you may prophesy.*
>
> *1 Cor. 14:1 NKJV*

Prophesy is especially important because the Word of God must be spoken into every situation. Prophecy is the gift that makes all the others work. Prophecy will make faith work. It will cause miracles to happen. It corrects and encourages us when necessary. Prophecy may be a Bible verse that comes to mind at an important time and gives the recipient hope and direction. Paul said that five words spoken in prophecy is better than ten thousand words in an unknown tongue (1Cor. 14:19): but that is if an interpreter is not present (1Cor. 27-28). This was not said to discourage speaking in tongues, as Paul also said:

> *I thank my God I speak with tongues more than you all;*
>
> *1 Cor. 14:18 NKJV*

Anyone reading and believing 1 Corinthians 12-14 should no longer be ignorant concerning Spiritual gifts. I have attempted to give a brief explanation on the gifts and to expound on them. If after reading the Word of God one still chooses to be ignorant on the gifts, the Holy Spirit has a Word for that person in ending chapter 14:

> *But if anyone is ignorant, let him be ignorant. Therefore, brethren, desire earnestly to prophesy, and do not forbid to speak with tongues. Let all things be done decently and in order.*
>
> *1 Cor. 14:38-40 NKJV*

Chapter 21

AUTHORITY AND POWER

⤳

The indwelling and the anointing of the Holy Spirit can be likened to that of granting authority and power to the Christian. When the Holy Spirit comes into a person, that person then is granted authority as a believer. Certain rights, privileges and duties are given him. When the Holy Spirit comes upon that believer, the Christian then has the power to carry out the authority.

In the King James Version and the New King James Version, the word power is often used when the word more accurately would be authority. If you look in a concordance, you will find that to be the case. Most modern translations properly distinguish the two words. Such is the case with the NASB, NIV, RSV, NRSV, and the NLT. We get a better understanding of the passages when we see the two words differentiated.

Jesus said in Matthew 28:18 in the KJV:

All power is given unto me in heaven and in earth.

The Greek word for power in this passage is *exousia*. The word properly translates to privilege or authority and is correctly translated that way in the above modern translations. Jesus was given all authority, and then told us to exercise that authority and to go and make disciples.

> *But as many as received him, to them gave he power to become the sons of God, even to them that believe on his name:*
>
> *John 1:12 KJV*

The word power is again translated properly as authority. As believers we *all* have authority, rights, and privileges as God's children. This does not mean that all share in His power. The Greek word for power is *dunamis*, the word from which dynamite is derived. This Greek word is properly translated in the KJV and the others.

> *But you shall receive power when the Holy Spirit has come upon you;*
>
> *Acts 1:8a NKJV*

Here the Lord was telling his disciples who already had the authority, that they would receive *power* when the Holy Spirit came upon them. These average Christians were filled with dynamite! When Paul laid his hands upon the Ephesian believers in Acts 19, they were filled with dynamite also. They then had the power to accomplish the duties the right and authority demanded.

Here is an illustration. If I were to drive down the street and a man stood next to the street and put out his hand to signal me to stop, I could drive right by him at 30 miles per hour. The man had no authority to stop me. But if that same man had a uniform on, with a badge prominently displayed, I would stop immediately. Why? Because he has full authority granted him by a higher authority to stop me. He represents the full authority of the municipality. If needed, he could pull out his .45 pistol and demonstrate the power! He has both power and authority. He has the badge which shows the authority, but he also has the dynamite! Many Christians have the badge but not the dynamite. You can have the authority without the power.

I have a driver's license granted me by my state. This gives me the authority to drive, but doesn't mean I have a car. I also have a gun owner's card, which gives me the authority to own guns and purchase ammunition. That doesn't mean I have any guns though.

In conclusion, we need the indwelling Holy Spirit for our authority as believers, and we need the filling, the baptism, or the anointing of the Holy Spirit to have the power. God the Father, the Son, and the Holy Spirit wants us to have both. As a body of believers and as individuals, we need to receive authority and power to operate in the sphere God has put us. After telling the Ephesian Christians to be filled with the Spirit, he told them to pray in the Holy Spirit.

Pray at all times and on every occasion in the power of the Holy Spirit. Stay alert and be persistent in your prayers for all Christians everywhere.
Ephesians 6:18 NLT

To my readers I end with the final chapter of the Word of God.

The Spirit and the bride say, "Come." Let each one who hears them say, "Come." Let the thirsty ones come-anyone who wants to. Let them come and drink the water of life without charge.
Revelation 22:17 NLT

EPILOGUE

I hope this book has helped you learn more of the Holy Spirit's relationship to you, the believer. It is my desire that you will continue the never ending quest for knowledge of the Holy Spirit of God. Books that I recommend and have helped me grow in the knowledge are the following:

The Baptism of the Holy Spirit, by R. A. Torrey, Bethany House Publishers, ISBN 0-87123-029-1.

The Person And Work Of The Holy Spirit, by R. A. Torrey, Zondervan Publishing House, ISBN 0-310-33301-6.

The Spirit Himself, by Ralph M. Riggs, Gospel Publishing House, ISBN 0-88243-590-6.

Secret Power, by Dwight L. Moody, Regal Books, ISBN 0-8307-1219-4.

The Holy Spirit And His Gifts, by Kenneth E. Hagin, Rhema Bible Church, AKA Kenneth Hagin Ministries, Inc. ISBN 0-89276-085-0.

Wesley Spiritual Gifts Questionnaire, by Donald Hohensee, Fuller Seminary Press.

> *But ye shall receive power, after that the Holy Ghost is come upon you: and ye shall be witnesses unto me both in Jerusalem, and in all Judea, and in Samaria, and unto the uttermost part of the earth.*
>
> *Acts 1:8*

Dr. James Warner has Bachelor of Science and Doctor of Chiropractic degrees. He received his Diploma in Pastoral Studies from the Southern Baptist Seminaries. He was born again in 1974, and became active in ministry shortly thereafter. Dr. Warner has taught different methods of evangelism: Evangelism Explosion, Transferable Concepts, Encounter Method, Roman Road, and the Great Commission School. He has taught the subjects of soul winning, prayer, and spiritual objectives throughout Illinois. He has witnessed in various places of the world, and has been on numerous Bible distributions around the country.

Dr. Warner is married to Janet, who also is active in the various ministries. He and Janet have four grown children: Lisa, Ken, Erika, and Sarah. The whole family (including the children's' spouses) is active in spreading the Gospel of Jesus Christ.

Dr. Warner can be reached at jwarner@warnerchiro.com. *The Handgun of the Holy Ghost, Understanding the Spirit of God* will do just as the name implies. Dr. Warner uses the Word of God to give a theological basis for the many experiences he has had with the Holy Spirit. Experience the personal adventure he shares when placed in jail and witness the Holy Spirit move mightily as scores are brought to salvation. Learn how to defend the faith against cultists who attempt to negate the Spirit of God. Receive *power* from on high when the Holy Spirit comes upon you-the reader.

All this you will find in *The Handgun of the Holy Ghost, Understanding the Spirit of God.*

Dr. Warner is available to speak at conferences and churches, teaching on the topics of the Holy Spirit, witnessing, soul winning, and natural health. He can be reached at: jwarner@warnerchiro.com.

Printed in the United States
67269LVS00002B/307-456

9 781600 348419